Oct 2

Lee

you are such an

encourager — thanks.

Jim

The ONE YEAR® MINI FOR Leaders

The ONE YEAR® MINI

FOR Leaders

TYNDALE HOUSE PUBLISHERS, INC.
CAROL STREAM, ILLINOIS

Visit Tyndale's exciting Web site at www.tyndale.com

TYNDALE and Tyndale's quill logo are registered trademarks of Tyndale House Publishers, Inc.

The One Year is a registered trademark of Tyndale House Publishers, Inc.

The One Year Mini for Leaders

Copyright © 2007 by Jim Seybert. All rights reserved.

Designed by Beth Sparkman

Edited by Linda Schlafer

Published in association with the literary agency of Mark Sweeney & Associates, Bonita Springs, Florida 34135.

Scripture quotations are taken from the *Holy Bible,* New Living Translation, copyright © 1996, 2004. Used by permission of Tyndale House Publishers, Inc., Carol Stream, Illinois 60188. All rights reserved.

ISBN-13: 978-1-4143-1188-3
ISBN-10: 1-4143-1188-5

Printed in China

13   12   11   10   09   08   07
7   6   5   4   3   2   1

DEDICATION

To my dad, a living example of a man whose reach exceeds his grasp.

THANKS AND ACKNOWLEDGMENTS

O for a thousand tongues to sing my thanks and gratitude to God for allowing me to experience the incredible blessings of this project. I have never worked so hard, nor felt God's presence so certainly.

My wife, Rhonda, and daughter, Noelle, sacrificed a lot during the six months when this book was being written, because I was frequently gone—both physically and mentally—as the pages came to life. My words are better because of their patience, love, and support.

I could always count on my mom for an encouraging word. She said she "got teary eyed" over a couple of my stories.

A handful of people tossed ideas around with me when I got stuck. Thanks to Andy Butcher, Andy Hyde, Joe Bubar, Jim Seybert Sr., John Seybert, Joe Brown, Eric Grimm, Fred Frank, Bob Turner, and Tom Buckles.

My agent and friend, Mark Sweeney, kept my head straight. Jon Farrar and Ron Beers at Tyndale House shared the vision and gave me a long leash.

Finally, I thank and acknowledge the people who have passed through my life, providing experiences that became examples for this book. Some are mentioned by name in the stories. Others are woven into the fabric of compiled stories, but all are part of God's great plan for my life. Only he knows what tomorrow has in store—I can hardly wait to find out.

INTRODUCTION

All truth is God's truth. He is the foundation of all truth.

This book will remind you of some basic leadership lessons by drawing connections between the truth God placed in Scripture and the experiences we've all had in leading companies and organizations.

Although I do believe that God is complex enough to weave tertiary levels of truth into his words, the daily lessons are not intended to challenge standard interpretations of biblical passages, as if to suggest, "This is what God *really* wanted to say."

To write this book, I simply read the Scriptures and noted each passage that reminded me of a leadership lesson I have learned during a career of more than thirty years in a variety of professions.

May God strengthen your relationship with him. He cares deeply about your professional life and wants to bless you more than you could possibly hope or imagine.

HOW TO USE THIS BOOK

Where space allows, I've included some background information to bring the daily Scripture passage into perspective, but you may want to have a Bible handy to read a few verses before and after the selected verses to provide greater context.

The Bible is a dynamic compilation of God's message to everyone. That certain passages are not relevant to you at the particular time you read them doesn't negate their truth, but makes the point that God is bigger—much bigger—than your individual perspective.

Finally, I guarantee that God will reward you for diligently seeking him. So, have a great year exploring his truth.

Jim Seybert
http://www.jimseybert.com

Do Something

In the beginning God created.   *GENESIS 1:1*

The first sentence of the Bible introduces us to one of God's notable characteristics. In the beginning, God did something.

He didn't think, study, see, feel, or plan. He created.

He didn't wait for the heavens and the earth to fall into place. He didn't assume they would feel empowered to create themselves. He didn't delegate the task to his assistant. The text is very clear—God created.

God took action and did things on his timeline in the way he wanted them done.

Sometimes you and I need to step up to the plate and swing the bat. There's a time for waiting and a time for doing. In our desire to strike a balance, we often fail to act in a timely manner. We wait for one more opinion or one last focus group when we know that we should move, now!

Perhaps you're facing something today that just needs to be tackled. Look to Genesis 1:1 for encouragement.

❖ *When the time was right, God stepped through the front door of time and did something.*

Communicate

When the people saw how long it was taking Moses to come back down the mountain, they gathered around Aaron. "Come on," they said, "make us some gods who can lead us. We don't know what happened to this fellow Moses, who brought us here from the land of Egypt."

EXODUS 32:1

You embody your organization's vision. When the staff sees you, they see the vision. When you're away, they begin to lose sight of where they are headed. This can happen very quickly.

Make it a practice to keep your staff updated from wherever you are. If you are attending a conference or convention, send an e-mail every evening to the entire staff, giving them a glimpse of what you are learning.

Don't manage from the road. You have subordinates at the office who can do that. Instead, learn as much as you can at the conference or convention. When you return, you can use the opportunity to tell your staff how the things you learned fit with your mission statement and share your thoughts about how new ideas might be applied.

❖ *Be out of sight, but not out of mind.*

Be Yourself

What do you benefit if you gain the whole world
but are yourself lost or destroyed?   *LUKE 9:25*

God made you. He knit you together in your
mother's womb, and before time began, he had a
plan for you. He designed your personality and gave
you your talents. You were created with a specific
purpose in God's mind.

God created the *self* that you are.

I am happiest when I'm living the life God planned
for me, using the personality and talents he gave me.
In other words, I'm happiest when I am being myself.

Conversely, I am most miserable when I barter a
portion of my God-given self for short-term earthly
gain.

This question from Jesus—"What do you benefit
if you gain the whole world but are yourself lost or
destroyed?"—is quite often used in a spiritual context, but you can use it to evaluate career decisions
as well.

Are you living the life God intended for you? Are
you using the talents and personality he gave you?
Are you being yourself?

❖ *Self-regard is not always a bad thing, especially if you're protecting the self God gave you.*

Play Fair

They refuse to understand, break their promises, are heartless, and have no mercy. . . . Worse yet, they encourage others to do [these things], too. *ROMANS 1:31-32*

"God shows his anger from heaven against all sinful, wicked people," writes Paul in Romans 1:18.

He describes all sorts of vile conduct—wickedness, murder, sexual perversion—that you'd expect to see under the heading of "Stuff God Hates." Then he concludes with four types of behavior that are common in the business world:

✦ Refusal to understand: *My mind is made up. It's my way or the highway.*
✦ Breaking of promises: *I know you were counting on it, but we gave Bob the promotion.*
✦ Heartlessness: *It's not personal; it's business. We need to make a profit.*
✦ Lack of mercy: *Nothing short of perfection is good enough.*

Profit earned at the expense of someone's family is greed.
Promises that can never be fulfilled are lies.
Stubborn refusal to consider new ideas is pride.

❖ *As a leader, treat your team as God would if he were their boss.*

Don't Waste Time

When Saul returned to his home . . . a group of men whose hearts God had touched went with him. But there were some scoundrels who complained, "How can this man save us?" And they scorned him and refused to bring him gifts. But Saul ignored them.   *1 SAMUEL 10:26-27*

Some people in your circle of influence are draining your organization of its vitality.

They are wasting your time and casting doubt on your decisions.

They are scoundrels and complainers who constantly question your motives and hamper your ability to lead.

Here's some good news: You have God's permission to ignore them.

At this point in his life, Saul was walking with God. He had a group of godly advisors as he began his reign as Israel's first king.

There is no evidence that God was upset with Saul for ignoring the people who scorned him and refused to honor his leadership. Paying attention to such people eventually caused him a lot of grief.

You know who these people are, so steer clear of them.

❖ *Not every voice is worth listening to. Don't let scoundrels waste your time.*

Plant Your Crop

Does a farmer always plow and never sow? Is he forever cultivating the soil and never planting?
ISAIAH 28:24

My wife is from a family of farmers in Nebraska. My father-in-law, Ken, spends a lot of time each spring working the soil. The fields look great when he's finished.

You could put everything I know about farming into a very small bucket, but I have figured out one thing: *You have to plant seeds if you expect to harvest anything in the fall.*

If all Ken did was plow the dirt, he'd have some really great-looking dirt.

Nothing is certain for farmers, but the yield is related to the amount and quality of the seeds they plant.

Have your harvests been less than you expected lately? Could you be spending too much time getting things ready? Is it time to put away the plow and start sowing seeds?

In Isaiah 28:26, the prophet concludes, "The farmer knows just what to do." I'm sure you do too.

❖ *If you want a harvest, you must put some good seeds in the ground.*

Play It Straight

Even my prophets and priests are like that. . . .
They give assurances of peace when there is no
peace.   *JEREMIAH 8:10-11*

I was managing a small business for absentee owners
who had made some unwise financial decisions. Cash
flow had dried up. Sales were on the rise, but we
couldn't meet our obligations.

My bosses wanted me to keep a happy face and lie
about our dire straits as they tried to finagle their way
out of the mess they had created, but I couldn't lie to
my staff.

I called them together and laid it out in plain English. Paychecks might be late. Benefits such as coffee
and free sodas were over. It wasn't pretty.

I also told them that we could work hard and pull
off a miracle despite the albatross around our necks.
And they agreed.

Since I was up-front with them and didn't give
"assurances of peace when there [was] no peace," the
staff was willing to go the extra miles needed to get
the business back on track—and we did it.

❖ *Always give it to them straight.*

Keep Moving Forward

Then Moses led the people of Israel away from the Red Sea.   *EXODUS 15:22*

Here's a sad paradox:

Success breeds failure.

The company had enjoyed a few years of stellar growth. An aggressive public relations campaign had positioned them as their industry's dominant player.

To cut costs, the executive team decided to scale back and allow the firm's reputation to speak for itself.

Within two years, the company was the subject of some very damaging rumors about their motives for a controversial new product line. Longtime customers were leaving, staff morale hit rock bottom, and the company's leaders were forced into crisis communication mode.

The new product was actually quite good, but an anemic PR effort had left too many unanswered questions, and negative perceptions had filled the void.

Moses knew that crossing the Red Sea wasn't an end in itself, and he quickly directed the people's attention toward the future.

❖ *Incremental success is not the ultimate objective. Once you successfully cross the Red Sea, take a moment to mark the occasion, then fix your sights on your destination and keep moving forward.*

Ask for What You Need

The leaders of the tribe of Levi came to consult with Eleazar the priest, Joshua son of Nun, and the leaders of the other tribes of Israel. They came to them at Shiloh in the land of Canaan and said, "The LORD commanded Moses to give us towns to live in and pasturelands for our livestock." *JOSHUA 21:1-2*

I was mentoring a bright young man in his first organizational-leadership role. He became frustrated when his board of directors allocated staff increases to every department but his.

I asked what the board had said when he requested the increase. He said, "I never actually asked. I just figured they knew how important this was. I mean, they're always talking about how much we need to grow."

It was common knowledge that the Levites would be given property within each of the other tribes' regional land grants.

Joshua, the Levites, and all the people knew this, but the Levites didn't just assume that Joshua would do what was right. They made their request.

My student had committed a common leadership error: He *presumed* and was not proactive with his requests. The board had committed to a growth strategy that included his department, but he had not followed through.

❖ *Never presume. Always ask.*

Trust God's Plan

Let us not become conceited, or provoke one another, or be jealous of one another.

GALATIANS 5:26

Why do we cheer for the underdogs?

They struggle to reach the next rung on the ladder and constantly feel the pressure of being a step behind. These perennial holders of honorable-mention trophies have chronic jealousy over other people's success.

It is easy to criticize those who brag about their accomplishments. We frown on bullies who inflame unhealthy situations, but we tend to condone feelings of jealousy because we have an intrinsic desire to see the underdog come out on top.

Paul ties these three traits together because God has uniquely created each of us for a specific purpose. If everything you have comes from God, you have no right to be conceited, no warrant for being a bully, and no reason to crave what you don't have.

❖ *Do your best for God, and be satisfied that he has a plan chosen especially for you, even if you're an underdog.*

Celebrate Success

Then Moses and the people of Israel sang this
song to the LORD. *EXODUS 15:1*

It was the middle of the week, about two or three
in the afternoon. Everyone in our little company
of twenty employees was busy doing what they did,
when the boss broke our concentration by walking
through the office and asking everyone to join him
in the accounting department.

When we arrived, he was standing in front of a
table filled with cake and ice cream. "We are celebrating today," he said, "because accounting has
just closed the books on our company's first-ever
one-million-dollar month."

He thanked us all for our part in making the
company successful and, as he often did, shared his
dreams for the future.

When was the last time you bought everyone
lunch, declared "Jeans Day" in the middle of the
week, or got the team together to publicly congratu-
late someone for a job well done?

❖ *People love being part of something that's
working, and they like pleasant surprises.*

Share Your Heart

People judge by outward appearance, but the LORD looks at the heart. *1 SAMUEL 16:7*

The CEO was frustrated. His company's best customers weren't signing up for a comprehensive new program that offered many excellent benefits. Many of them threatened to take their business elsewhere.

"Don't they know that I want them to succeed?" he asked.

"They can't know unless you tell them," I answered.

"But I just assumed they'd know my heart."

Your customers, your staff, and even your closest friends won't know your heart unless you tell them. If you're assuming they will somehow just know your intentions, you will be disappointed.

Samuel was choosing a new king for Israel. If he relied only on what he could see, he would make the wrong choice in this important decision.

The CEO shared his heart in a letter to his customers, and many of them signed up for the new program. One wrote, "I just needed to hear it from your heart."

❖ *Are you waiting for someone to make an important choice? Have you told them how you feel about it?*

Love Justice

Be just and fair to all. Do what is right and good. *ISAIAH 56:1*

Ron made a killing in the dot-com boom and invested a lot of his own money in an Internet venture that grew much more slowly than anyone expected. The business is healthy now, but the early stages were very tough at times.

When he faced some extremely difficult layoffs, Ron eliminated his own salary in order to keep a few more people on the payroll.

I asked what had led him to that decision. He said, "I can find other sources of income. This is all that some of these people have. It was the right thing to do."

Is it fair to pay executive bonuses while hourly staff does without the additional help they need? Is it "right and good" to lay off people on the day you take delivery of a new plasma-screen TV?

How do you justify unfair practices? What reasons do you have for not doing what is right?

❖ *When was the last time you took a bullet for your team?*

Excite Their Emotions

Jesus called out to them, "Come, follow me, and I will show you how to fish for people!"
MATTHEW 4:19

The success of a marketing campaign depends on the degree to which you can excite the emotions of the people you are trying to reach.

It's not enough to give them the facts about your product or service; you have to touch their hearts, ignite a passion. Your goal should be to create a desire for your vision and make them *want* it, even if they don't believe they *need* it.

Peter and Andrew were fishermen whose lives revolved around fishing. In those days, fishing wasn't a job, but a lifestyle.

Jesus was a master at knowing what was important to people's hearts. As he walked along the shore, he had probably even watched Peter and Andrew work their father's boat.

"Did you hear that, Andrew? He says he'll teach us a whole new way to fish—let's go!"

Whenever you need people to follow you, find a way to excite their emotions.

❖ *Create a desire, not just a need.*

Ask God

You don't have what you want because you don't ask God for it.   *JAMES 4:2*

A friend of mine tells a story that drives home the power of making your requests known.

"Our goal was to raise three million dollars for the church building program.

"We visited all of our church members to enlist their support. We never specifically asked for contributions, but we did ask them to prayerfully consider their involvement.

"One church member was a very wealthy gentleman who was known for his generosity. On Pledge Sunday, this man handed me a check for fifty thousand dollars.

"I was overwhelmed. Then, about six months later, the local paper ran a photo of this man giving a one-million-dollar check to the YMCA.

"I wanted to know why he hadn't done the same for his own church, so I made an appointment and asked him, point blank, 'Why did you pledge fifty thousand dollars to your church and a million to the YMCA?'"

"I'll never forget his answer: 'You didn't ask for it, and the YMCA did.'"

❖ *Do you not have what you want because you haven't asked for it?*

Plan Your Moves

If it please the king, let the king and Haman
come today to a banquet I have prepared for the
king.   *ESTHER 5:4*

Esther's story is one of my favorites, especially the
chess game that unfolds as Esther sets Haman up for
a stunning reversal of fortune at King Xerxes' hands.

As queen, Esther could have spoken directly to
Xerxes about the lies Haman was telling, but she
chose to host a series of banquets and seated Haman
in the place of honor beside the king.

Instead of jumping to her desired conclusion, as in
a game of checkers, Esther orchestrated the conversation so that Xerxes would reach a "checkmate" conclusion and seal the verdict against Haman.

As a leader, you will sometimes have the opportunity to push through an agenda and "run the check-
erboard," but that's not always the best long-term
strategy.

❖ *Consider the countermoves you might face,
and plan your game with the skill of a chess
master, like Queen Esther.*

Focus on the Mission

The king said, "What should I do to honor a man who truly pleases me?" Haman thought to himself, "Whom would the king wish to honor more than me?" *ESTHER 6:6*

This Haman fellow was one incredible piece of work. He was the king's closest advisor, but instead of focusing on the king's needs, he was consumed with himself and wound up in an inescapable corner.

Leadership requires a measure of self-assurance. Being able to say, "Follow me" takes personal confidence in your decisions and faith in your abilities. God created your ego, and having a healthy ego is a good thing.

Haman got in trouble because he regarded his own agenda as more important than his job of serving the king. He manipulated the king's resources to his personal benefit, ultimately to the expense of the mission. In the end, this cost him everything.

❖ *Evaluate your motives and objectives. Do your decisions benefit the mission, or just your personal agenda? Stay focused on the mission, and your ego will be under control.*

Dream Big Dreams

As he slept, [Jacob] dreamed of a stairway that reached from the earth up to heaven. And he saw the angels of God going up and down the stairway.   *GENESIS 28:12*

"Man's reach should exceed his grasp."

This line from a Robert Browning poem hung on our garage wall when I was growing up, and my dad still lives its truth. He is always reaching beyond his grasp to try something new, always looking for another ladder to climb.

I don't think he has ever sought a leadership position, but folks just flock to whatever he's doing. His enthusiasm is contagious because he dreams *big*—bigger than anyone else I know.

God was about to take his covenant with Abraham's offspring to a dramatic new level, so he gave Jacob a dream that would exceed his grasp by about 10,000 percent. This was the most fantastic vision anyone on earth had ever seen.

The power of this dream would sustain Jacob through some tough stuff on the horizon, just as your dreams for the future will strengthen you.

❖ *Let your dreams stretch you.*

Hire Good People

Moses' arms soon became so tired he could no longer hold them up. So Aaron and Hur found a stone for him to sit on. Then they stood on each side of Moses, holding up his hands.   *EXODUS 17:12*

This is a great story. As long as Moses kept his hands in the air, the Israelite army succeeded in their battle against the Amalekites. Aaron and Hur saw that Moses was getting tired, so they supported him by literally lending a hand.

Aaron and Hur showed respect for their leader, but there is also a lesson about Moses in all of this.

Moses hired good people.

A leader's effectiveness often results from the people he or she has hired. Getting good people on your team is a major step toward achieving your mission. Look for people who can complement your own skills and talents.

❖ *Recruit to your own weaknesses, and enjoy the support you receive when you need it most.*

Appreciate Your Supporters

Some of the Pharisees said, "This man Jesus is not from God, for he is working on the Sabbath." Others said, "But how could an ordinary sinner do such miraculous signs?" So there was a deep division of opinion among them.   *JOHN 9:16*

If people were confused about Jesus, what makes you think you can get them to understand you?

The Pharisees were smart guys. They knew Jewish law, and they were *very* particular about obeying its tiniest detail. For the Pharisees, there wasn't a lot of gray area. You did what the law said, or else.

Despite their deep knowledge of Mosaic law, the Pharisees were divided as to whether or not Jesus had violated the Sabbath. I'm going to suggest they didn't understand because they didn't *want* to understand.

The lesson from this passage is that you will never get everyone to agree with you. Jesus focused his attention on the people who *would* engage with his message. He was looking for the handful of people who would give him 100 percent of their support.

❖ *Don't waste your time trying to get 100 percent participation from 100 percent of the people. It's not going to happen.*

Follow Christ's Example

Imitate God, therefore, in everything you do, because you are his dear children. Live a life filled with love, following the example of Christ.
EPHESIANS 5:1-2

Everyone who worked in our sales department was required to attend a weeklong intensive seminar called Sales Boot Camp. The school was run by a feisty little guy who inspired students to go home and *sell, sell, sell.*

As a young salesman, I was motivated to follow his lead until I asked some questions about the teacher's experience and discovered that he was all smoke and no fire. The guy had never actually sold anything, and some places he had managed had gone bankrupt under his direction. I did not want to reproduce his history.

Imitating God is a different matter.

Paul confidently suggested that you follow Christ's example because he knew that Jesus had been there and done that.

Jesus exhibited incredible leadership skills. He was decisive and compassionate, visionary and grounded, focused and flexible.

❖ *First, imitate God. Then leave a credible example for the people who follow you.*

Take Charge

Israel's leaders took charge, and the people gladly followed. Praise the LORD! *JUDGES 5:2*

Israel was a disaster. They had been under the control of King Jabin of Hazor, who had ruthlessly oppressed them for twenty years. God raised the prophetess Deborah as a judge to lead them in a decisive defeat of Jabin and his army.

On the final day of battle, Deborah sang a song that began with this verse about Israel's leaders taking charge.

There are two types of leaders—those who lead and those who don't.

People are looking for someone to lead them. When Israel's leaders took charge and actually started leading, the people gladly followed.

Being in a leadership position is only part of the equation. People are hungry for vision and direction. These often come from an unexpected source. God found Deborah sitting under a tree at the edge of town.

If no one is following, are you really leading?

❖ Look around you. Are people in your organization waiting for someone to step up and take control?

What's Your Next Goal?

After that generation died, another generation grew up who did not acknowledge the LORD or remember the mighty things he had done for Israel. *JUDGES 2:10*

A dominant Old Testament theme is the people's on-again, off-again relationship with God. In this instance, Joshua had just died, and there was no apparent leader to take his place.

The Israelites had finally reached the land they had been promised, and their focus had shifted from wilderness survival to inhabiting the land. They were ready to grow into the nation God had promised Abram hundreds of years earlier.

Their lives were easier now than at any time since they had entered Egypt under Joseph's supervision. They weren't scrambling for manna every morning; they were building towns and clearing fields. Things were looking good.

They had succeeded and had begun to coast.

As a leader, keep your eye on the next challenge. Celebrate when your team reaches an objective, and then help them focus on the next goal.

❖ *What's next for your organization? What will your focus be when current goals are achieved?*

Don't Be Sidetracked

"Should we pull out the weeds?" they asked. "No," he replied, "you'll uproot the wheat if you do. Let both grow together until the harvest."

MATTHEW 13:28-30

I had just cleaned my windshield and was heading out on a long trip when a big bug splattered onto it. I pulled off and cleaned the windshield. Within minutes, another bug hit and I stopped again.

Clean—Drive—Splat—Stop.

This continued until it was time to turn around and head home. I never made it to my destination, but I had a clean windshield the entire trip.

This ridiculous story emphasizes what happens when we take our eyes off the objective and let unimportant things slow us down.

Jesus used a parable to teach the importance of staying focused on the mission.

A farmer planted wheat. His enemies came in the night and planted weeds. The farmer let them both grow, because pulling the weeds might damage the wheat.

Are you drawn from your mission by petty annoyances that should be left alone?

❖ *Sometimes your best strategy is doing nothing at all.*

Consider New Ideas

Anyone who claims to know all the answers doesn't really know very much.   *1 CORINTHIANS 8:2*

In the mid-1970s, one in every three wristwatches sold worldwide was manufactured in Switzerland. By 1983, that ratio had dropped to one in ten.

Swiss watchmakers believed that the public wouldn't buy inexpensive digital watches flooding the market from Japan and elsewhere. They were wrong.

This was a classic example of self-deception.

Yesterday's knowledge does not solve tomorrow's problems.

Paul was helping the church at Corinth to see that some of their religious practices were rooted in long-standing tradition rather than in divine truth. He realized that knowledge made them feel important and urged them to consider new ways of thinking.

You can't afford to make leadership decisions based only on old knowledge or tradition. The best way to avoid costly errors in judgment is to realize you don't know everything. When someone comes along with a fresh idea, listen.

❖ *Admitting that your current knowledge base is outdated doesn't mean you've been wrong, only that things have changed and you need an update.*

Honor the Past

In the future your children will ask you, "What do these stones mean?" Then you can tell them, "They remind us that the Jordan River stopped flowing when the Ark of the LORD's Covenant went across." *JOSHUA 4:6-7*

When I tell stories about my childhood, my daughter raises her hand to her forehead and pretends to peer into the distance. She makes fun of my tendency to repeat the same themes.

Reviewing the past provides a strong platform for future decisions.

Joshua instructed the people to have one person from each tribe bring a rock from the center of the river. These were fashioned into a memorial so that future generations could remember how God had helped them cross the river. That knowledge could then influence their view of the future.

A leader's attention belongs on what lies ahead. History is important because it provides a perspective for the future, but we don't live in the past.

❖ *There's a difference between living in history and learning from it. Which do you do most often?*

Establish Common Bonds

Your bodies will bear the mark of my everlasting
covenant. *GENESIS 17:13*

God recruited Abraham to lead a new nation and
devised a common identifying mark for all the men.

There's great value in establishing common bonds
among your team members. Doing so provides a
dual benefit: Your team will be identified to outsiders
as sharing a common objective, and individual team
members will feel a kinship with one another.

There should be something about your organization that says, "We're in this together." It should
be more than a common uniform or dress code,
although there's nothing wrong with that for certain
public events.

You're not looking for clones. The unifying mark
might be a certain attitude about the future, a unique
way of addressing success, or a commitment to innovation. You might ask your customers what common
traits they see in your people. Use their comments to
talk to the staff about their common mark of unity.

❖ *What's your organization's common mark of
unity?*

Maintain Your Standards

His wife said to him, "Are you still trying to maintain your integrity? Curse God and die." But Job replied, "You talk like a foolish woman. Should we accept only good things from the hand of God?" *JOB 2:9-10*

It is tempting to relax your standards when situations turn against you.

Under increased competition, an organization may reduce the quality of its product to gain margin. A long waiting list can tempt restaurants to rush people who came for a relaxed meal. Politicians who are elected on a reform platform may change their positions when they learn that real influence requires going along with the old guard.

Job's wife was one of many who encouraged him to ignore his commitments. Their arguments were logical and well intentioned.

But Job's mission was to serve God. He refused to cheapen his product, soften his employee benefit package, or reduce innovation and stick with old ideas.

❖ *The measure of a true leader is the way in which he or she handles core values and commitments when circumstances are beyond his or her control.*

Consider New Solutions

So the people of Israel walked through the middle of the sea on dry ground, with walls of water on each side! *EXODUS 14:22*

Reggie McNeal, author of *The Present Future*, says that God is a master of "Red Sea Moments." Reggie's explanation is that "God is forever finding a completely unique way to solve problems. He'd rather invent a new solution than go with something that's been done before."

Hungry?—I'll drop manna from heaven every morning.

Need to cross the Jordan at flood stage?—Watch this!

Five thousand hungry people to feed?—Where's the kid with a lunch box?

Leading means taking people to places they've never been before. Solving new problems with old answers is counter to the agenda.

Always look for Red Sea solutions before rolling out the old boat and floating across the water.

❖ *Next time your team is faced with a monumental problem, explain the concept of Red Sea solutions and challenge them to find a new way to part the water.*

Stay Engaged

Joshua kept holding out his spear until everyone who had lived in Ai was completely destroyed. *JOSHUA 8:26*

NFL coaches are fun to watch. These guys blow off more energy than their players during the game—running up and down the sidelines, shouting their lungs out, arguing with referees, throwing their headsets to the ground. There's no doubt the coach has his head in the game.

How strange would it be if the coach pulled up a chair, slipped on his earbuds, and started reading *Sports Illustrated* during the game? What if he left the field to take a phone call regarding a prospective player for next year's team?

The players in this ridiculous scenario would quickly lose heart, and their performance would slide.

As long as the soldiers saw that Joshua was engaged, they fought on.

Your people need to know that you are engaged in their battles. You may not be on the field, but you need to show an active interest in their progress.

❖ *Can your team tell that you are actively in the game?*

Envision the Future

The neighbor women said, "Now at last Naomi has a son again!" And they named him Obed. He became the father of Jesse and the grandfather of David.   *RUTH 4:17*

Naomi's son married Ruth and then died. Because Naomi had no male offspring to care for her, she returned to her native people to live out her days. Ruth had every right to stay in her hometown and remarry, but she decided to go with her mother-in-law.

In Naomi's hometown, Ruth met a man who wanted to marry her, and he went through the proper steps to do so. They had a child who had a child who had a child who became King David, into whose bloodline Jesus was born—and you know the rest of that story.

Wow!

Do you regularly step out of the present to brainstorm the future results of your current decisions? Based on what you are doing today, where might you be in ten years?

❖ *Choices you made yesterday are already affecting your future. Does that have an effect on decisions you'll make tomorrow?*

Cut Slackers Loose

Instead of worshiping the glorious, ever-living God, they worshiped idols made to look like mere people and birds and animals and reptiles. So God abandoned them to do whatever shameful things their hearts desired. *ROMANS 1:23-24*

Paul points to one of God's important leadership qualities:

God doesn't waste time.

Perhaps you've been struggling with an employee or customer who clearly doesn't get it.

You tell yourself that a little more effort will eventually pay off. You add up what you've already invested in strengthening the relationship and decide that it would be foolish to throw it all away.

Every situation is unique, and you may very well be on the brink of a breakthrough, but pay attention to how God handles similar circumstances.

He has an unlimited amount of time and infinite resources at his disposal, but he still abandons those who refuse to get with the program.

❖ *When the time comes to cut people loose, God cuts them loose. What are you waiting for?*

Do Your Part

If you think you are too important to help someone, you are only fooling yourself. You are not that important. *GALATIANS 6:3*

We had an early bird pass to a Disney World theme park and were standing with other guests waiting for a cast member to drop the rope and let us run like crazy to the popular rides.

As we stood in the sweltering morning humidity, a man dressed in a suit and carrying a briefcase scurried across the grounds in an obvious rush to get where he was going.

Suddenly he stopped, walked over to a garden area, bent down, and picked up a piece of paper lodged under a bush. He stuffed the trash in his pocket and continued on his way.

At Disney, it's *everyone's* job to keep the park clean. The guy in the suit was no less obligated to do so than the college intern who had just arrived.

Paul teaches that none of us are too important to do what needs to be done.

❖ *Do you have a bit of trash in your pocket?*

Do Your Research

He waited another seven days and then released the dove again. This time it did not come back. *GENESIS 8:12*

Imagine Noah's disappointment when the dove came back the first time with nothing in its beak. He had done his research, and it had failed—or had it?

It's my belief that properly conducted research is never a failure because you learn something even when the results are not what you expected. In fact, a survey that reveals an unexpected result is probably more successful than one that just confirms what you already knew.

Noah did not change his approach on the second and third attempts. He ran the research exactly the same all three times. Release the dove, wait for it to return, wait seven days, release the *same* dove, wait for it to return, release the *same* dove. Maintaining consistency throughout a research project adds a bulletproof level of credibility.

❖ *If you're facing a big decision and the data comes back with something unexpected, you haven't failed; you've merely taken another step toward success.*

Don't Fear Failure

The men of Ai chased the Israelites from the town gate as far as the quarries, and they killed about thirty-six who were retreating down the slope. *JOSHUA 7:4-5*

Scottish playwright Robert Burns is generally credited with coining the phrase that eventually became

> *The best laid plans of mice and men often go awry.*

Sometimes things just don't turn out the way we envision. In this case, Joshua's troops suffered their first defeat. This happened because of one man's sin. He had collected spoils from a previous battle and kept them for himself against God's specific orders.

After the sin had been eradicated, Joshua led his soldiers back to Ai and soundly defeated them.

Failure doesn't always mean the objective is wrong. Football teams don't score every time they get the ball, but their objective never changes. There's almost always more than one solution to a problem.

❖ *Perhaps a team you're leading has suffered a series of setbacks. Before you question your goals, take a critical look at the methods you're using to achieve them.*

Be Consistent

You have done what you promised, for you are
always true to your word. *NEHEMIAH 9:8*

When you have time, read the ninth chapter of
Nehemiah. In this wonderful prayer, the Israelites
recounted the many ways in which God had shown
his faithfulness to them since the beginning of time.

Consistency is another of God's leadership attributes we should emulate.

God's methods are often unusual (the Red Sea,
manna, Calvary), but his focus and mission always
remain the same. As Nehemiah described him, "the
great and mighty and awesome God . . . keeps his
covenant of unfailing love" (Nehemiah 9:32).

The Israelites never questioned God's response
to their frequent and regular sin. They understood
and even expected the punishment he handed out.
Nor were they surprised when he forgave and healed
them.

They had come to depend on his consistency.

Do your people know how you will respond in
every situation? Do you stay on an even keel, or are
people sometimes caught off guard by your reactions
to circumstances?

❖ *Is your leadership style fair and balanced or
arbitrary and volatile?*

Expect Something New

But forget all that—it is nothing compared to what I am going to do. For I am about to do something new. *ISAIAH 43:18-19*

History defines who we are, and past experience is a good predictor of future results. To understand what will happen tomorrow, study what happened yesterday.

The Israelites put great stock in their past. Hebrew kids could recite oral histories all the way back to Adam.

Their fixation on history became a problem, however.

They took their eyes off the future. They didn't look beyond the horizon because they liked where they had been and where they were. They wanted the future to be just like the past.

As the book of Isaiah unfolds, God promises a victory. The Israelites thought it would be a military or political victory because of how God had led them before.

God said, "Forget all that." His future would involve something new.

❖ Perhaps your organization has focused too much on its history. What worked before may not work tomorrow. Is it time to "forget all that" and do something new?

Express Your Preferences

Carefully determine what pleases the Lord.
EPHESIANS 5:10

I am facilitating an executive staff meeting with a team that is trying to solve a critical issue facing their company. They are sharp people, but they are crippled by the unplanned absence of their president.

Every suggestion is met with something like, "He won't like that."

This team had a very clear picture of what the boss disliked, but when I asked them to focus on what the boss *liked,* they came up empty.

It wasn't their fault. They had to practice "avoidance planning," because they only knew what they were not supposed to do and where they weren't supposed to go.

It's your duty to show your team what pleases you.

Give them a clear picture of what you want. For example,
"I'd like to see more of this."
"This is working; let's build on it."
"I wish we could have more of that."

❖ *Imagine being a taxi driver with passengers who only told you where they didn't want to go.*

Examine Your Motives

These people are grumblers and complainers, living only to satisfy their desires. They brag loudly about themselves, and they flatter others to get what they want.   *JUDE 1:16*

Warning!

To bring about change, it's necessary to challenge the status quo. Doing so can get you branded as a grumbler or complainer.

How do you lead an organization to a different future without being seen as a gadfly who is never satisfied?

The answer lies with your motives. Before suggesting a change, examine your own intentions:

- *Am I suggesting this change because of something I personally don't like?*
- *Will this change move us closer to our mission objective?*
- *Is there research to support my ideas, or am I relying on my own opinions?*

Jude began his letter by saying that he wanted to write about the common goals shared by the believers. He also felt the need to warn them against people who could sidetrack their mission by manipulating others to get what they wanted.

❖ *Are you trying to move your organization forward? Are your motives above reproach?*

Communicate Your Legacy

This is the written account of the descendants of Adam. *GENESIS 5:1*

I was employee number fourteen at a company that grew to have more than one hundred employees in less than three years.

Before long, people who had been with us less than a year outnumbered the old-timers, and that posed a problem.

The company's founder was a visionary, charismatic entrepreneur. Our first employees had a personal connection with the passion that drove him.

The recent hires did a great job, but their passion for our mission was missing. They knew where we were going, but they didn't know how we had gotten to where we were or what made us tick.

We asked some old-timers to design a company museum that captured our legacy. The result was a stream of passion that extended from the most senior to the most recent members of the team.

Moses kept a historical record so those who came later would know how they got to where they were.

❖ *Does your newest hire know how you got where you are today?*

Keep Looking Ahead

Jacob was terrified at the news. He divided his household, along with the flocks and herds and camels, into two groups. He thought, "If Esau meets one group and attacks it, perhaps the other group can escape." *GENESIS 32:7-8*

A friend who spends a lot of time in crowded airport terminals taught me to "bat walk."

Bats are virtually blind, so they send radar signals ahead of them. This allows them to fly through dense forests without hitting any branches.

Bat walking is the practice of walking through a crowded terminal or down a city sidewalk with your eyes scanning the crowd twenty to thirty feet ahead. By doing so, you can adjust your direction and flow through the sea of people with amazing smoothness.

Leadership also requires some bat walking.

By keeping your gaze far ahead of the immediate environment, you will be able to adjust to whatever comes your way.

❖ *Jacob looked ahead, saw what might be happening, and devised a plan before it was too late. You should too.*

Encourage the Troops

Then as I looked over the situation, I called together the nobles and the rest of the people and said to them, "Don't be afraid of the enemy!"
NEHEMIAH 4:14

A group of Boy Scouts struggled up a steep mountain trail. It was hot and dry, many of the boys had sore feet, some had empty canteens, and one or two were ready to sit down and cry. They were miserable.

The Scoutmaster was up ahead. He reached the summit and shouted, "Hey guys, I know you're tired and it's really hot, but there's an awesome lake just over the top. Have courage. Keep going."

Leaders have different perspectives from the people who follow them. It's easy to ignore the concerns of the group because you can see beyond the present, but it's your job to encourage them.

The Israelites were surrounded by enemy soldiers, and they were frightened. Nehemiah knew what the outcome would be. He had been to the mountaintop, so he could acknowledge their concerns and reassure them.

❖ *What can you see that your troops can't?*

Improve Your Community

When you give to someone in need, don't do as the hypocrites do—blowing trumpets in the synagogues and streets to call attention to their acts of charity! *MATTHEW 6:2*

Many organizations include "cause marketing" in their strategic plans. They donate money toward a charitable endeavor that is attractive to their core customers. This is often done with the best of intentions.

Priorities can go seriously awry, however, as in the case of a big corporation that donated one hundred thousand dollars to a popular charity and then spent two million dollars advertising their largesse.

You have to doubt their sincerity when they spent twenty times as much to pat themselves on the back. It may have been a great marketing campaign, but it was just wrong.

❖ *Whether you get any benefit from it or not, your organization should be doing something to improve your community. If you're not, give someone the assignment of finding a cause that makes sense to your staff and your customers. Support it to the best of your ability and "give your gifts in private" (Matthew 6:4).*

Notice What Is Important

Jesus realized at once that healing power had gone out from him, so he turned around in the crowd and asked, "Who touched my robe?"   *MARK 5:30*

Jesus had just arrived by boat, a large crowd had flocked to him, and a popular local pastor had asked him to heal his daughter when a sick woman touched his robe.

You can sense the pandemonium. People had heard about this man from Nazareth, and this was *their* chance to see him in action. The buzz, the excitement, and the noise were intense.

Even in the midst of this bedlam, Jesus knew that someone had intentionally touched his robe.

The disciples shook their heads. "You've got to be kidding. Look at all these people. They've *all* been touching you."

But Jesus had a leader's perspective. He had the ability to be in the moment without being consumed by it. He was filtering out the noise and paying attention to what was important.

Do you become caught in the moment, or do you sort through the rubble to see what's significant?

❖ *How good is your leadership filter?*

Redefine Success

Don't just pretend to love others. Really love them. Hate what is wrong. Hold tightly to what is good. Love each other with genuine affection, and take delight in honoring each other. Never be lazy, but work hard and serve the Lord enthusiastically. Rejoice in our confident hope. Be patient in trouble, and keep on praying. When God's people are in need, be ready to help them. Always be eager to practice hospitality.

Bless those who persecute you. Don't curse them; pray that God will bless them. Be happy with those who are happy, and weep with those who weep. Live in harmony. . . . Enjoy the company of ordinary people. And don't think you know it all!

Never pay back evil with more evil. Do things in such a way that everyone can see you are honorable. Do all that you can to live in peace with everyone. *ROMANS 12:9-18*

Is there a better foundation on which to build your organization's core values?

❖ *Ask your team to read this passage daily for a month. Ask God for new perspectives on measuring success.*

Defend against Rumors

I am telling you this so no one will deceive you with well-crafted arguments. *COLOSSIANS 2:4*

As I write this, residents and officials just outside of Yosemite National Park are dealing with a massive rock slide that has closed a main road into this popular vacation spot. The situation is serious. It could be over a year before the road reopens.

When the slide first occurred, everyone had their own spin on what was being done, and most of the stories were grossly exaggerated. Then a government employee began e-mailing a daily update to residents and community leaders.

Within days, the rumor mill had subsided, and people began talking about solutions.

Paul was away from the church at Colossae. He knew that human nature would fabricate rumors to fill gaps in the available information, so he made certain that they had what they needed to fight the rumor mill.

Do your people have enough information, or have you allowed the rumor mill to fabricate phony facts?

❖ *Perhaps you need to plan an information offensive and put rumors to rest before they get started.*

Treat People Well

"I am an Egyptian—the slave of an Amalekite," he replied. "My master abandoned me three days ago because I was sick. . . . If you take an oath in God's name that you will not kill me or give me back to my master, then I will guide you to them."
1 SAMUEL 30:13-15

Letting people go is never a pleasant experience. Regardless of the circumstances, you must treat them with respect.

David and his soldiers were chasing a band of Amalekites who had pillaged an Israelite city while David was away. They came across the Egyptian slave of an Amalekite who agreed to take them to his master in revenge for having been left in the desert to die.

David's sympathy for an enemy shows us how to treat people, regardless of their connection to us. The Amalekite's mistreatment of his servant—and the servant's subsequent revenge—is an example of the potential consequences of treating people disrespectfully, even as they are being dismissed.

❖ *You'll be treated the same way you treat others—is that okay with you?*

Learn Humility

Human pride will be brought down, and human arrogance will be humbled.   *ISAIAH 2:11*

There's an old country-and-western song that goes, "Oh Lord, it's hard to be humble, when you're perfect in every way . . ."

Here's a fact: The song is absolutely correct. Handling the fame that comes with a leadership role is one of the hardest lessons to learn.

By definition, leadership requires you to have a certain level of celebrity within your sphere of influence, whether it's large or small.

Your position will attract people for many reasons. Some will genuinely seek your leadership. Others will want to be near you because of what you can do for them.

God warned the Israelites that pride had turned them away from their mission, which was to obey him. Their leaders had strayed, and God was using Isaiah to help them understand the mess they had gotten into.

❖ *It is not difficult to develop an arrogant or prideful attitude. It's so easy that you often don't realize it until it's too late. How are you handling the leadership spotlight?*

Motivate Change

The serpent was the shrewdest of all the wild animals the Lord God had made. One day he asked the woman, "Did God really say you must not eat the fruit?" *GENESIS 3:1*

Contrary to your calling as a leader, most people are comfortable with leaving things just the way they are. I call it "organizational inertia."

Leadership involves change—and change is something that many people in your organization would like to avoid.

There are two ways to bring about change. You can force people to do something different (this is actually pushing, not leading), or you can create a desire in them for change.

Though his intentions were evil, the shrewd serpent exercised excellent leadership skills by getting Eve to question the status quo. He got her to imagine something better than she already had. He led her to her own conclusion and watched as she initiated the change he had in mind. No one forced Eve to eat the fruit.

❖ *If you see a need for change in your organization, find ways to challenge the status quo and give people a desire for something outside their comfort zones.*

Expect the Unexpected

There once was a man named Job who lived in the land of Uz. He was blameless—a man of complete integrity. He feared God and stayed away from evil.   *JOB 1:1*

Everyone knows Job's story. He's the guy who lost everything and displayed such an enduring spirit that we describe persevering people as having "the patience of Job."

Patience is a quality to which you should aspire, but let's look at another key element in the story:

Job was blameless.

Job did nothing to cause the calamity that befell him. Job played by the rules. He was a generous and respectable community member, a loving husband, a good father, and a smart businessman.

Many circumstances are beyond our control. You can—and should—plan for various scenarios, but always remember that

Stuff Happens.

Take time to review your current strategies. Is there room for adjustment along the way? Or will things fall apart if they don't go exactly according to plan?

❖ *Expect unexpected things to occur. Be flexible. Don't be surprised by surprises.*

Correct People Kindly

Daniel (also known as Belteshazzar) was overcome for a time, frightened by the meaning of the dream. . . . "I wish the events foreshadowed in this dream would happen to your enemies, my lord, and not to you!" *DANIEL 4:19*

My consulting assignments often involve fixing problems, and I am required to deliver negative reports to my clients. There is no pleasure in being the bearer of bad news—except that it eventually leads to corrective action—and I always preface my comments by saying, "This will be uncomfortable, but you paid me to tell you the truth, so here it is."

I've never feared for my life, as Daniel did, but our attitudes are similar. When you have bad news to deliver, do it with grace.

Don't pull punches or sugarcoat reality, but protect the feelings of the person receiving the report. Daniel knew that Nebuchadnezzar would endure seven years of insanity. He warned the king and urged him to take action to avoid calamity.

❖ *Decision makers need all the facts, both positive and negative.*

Share Good Results

What farmer plants a vineyard and doesn't have the
right to eat some of its fruit?   *1 CORINTHIANS 9:7*

Many organizations are compartmentalized to
the extent that someone may start a new project
and then never touch it after it passes to the next
development stage.

Human beings need closure; we like to know that
our contributions matter. We need to see and enjoy
the fruits of our labor.

Paul argued with those who criticized him for
expecting "a share of the harvest" (1 Corinthians
9:10). He reasoned that "the one who plows and the
one who threshes the grain" (v. 10) should reap some
benefits.

One effective method of sharing the outcome with
everyone in your organization is to provide regular
reports from end users of your product or service.
When someone writes in with a great compliment,
make sure the folks at the very beginning of the
development process hear how their original idea is
meeting someone's needs.

❖ *Look for ways to connect those at the begin-*
ning of an idea with those at the end. When the
team wins, find ways for everyone to attend the
victory celebration.

Value Negative Feedback

When troubles come your way, consider it an opportunity for great joy.   *JAMES 1:2*

Let's hear it for the complainers and perennial dark clouds who are part of every leader's life. If it weren't for these folks who go out of their way to tell you what's wrong, your leadership would suffer for lack of truthful input.

Most great ideas are born out of a desire to scratch an itch, right a wrong, or fix a problem. If you want to be the kind of leader who makes changes and carries the team forward, you'll need to look for nuggets of truth in the negative feedback that comes your way.

The CEO of a large retail chain reportedly walks onto the sales floor of his stores to ask employees and shoppers, "What do we do that's dumb?" I'm sure he learns a lot more from these answers than by asking, "What do you like about us?"

How long has it been since you spent time listening to the pessimists and naysayers?

❖ *Blessed are the grumblers, for they shall point out opportunities for change.*

Make the Difficult Decisions

If we hadn't wasted all this time, we could have gone and returned twice by now.   *GENESIS 43:10*

By all standards, it was a successful ministry—good attendance, dedicated staff, strong missional outreach, and a healthy budget.

But an elephant in the room was making everyone uncomfortable. The "Wednesday Night Family Meal Time" was not doing well. It had never done well. Attendance was bad, the food was second-rate, and the volunteer staff could have been assigned more effectively.

Although there were more effective programs to focus on, no one was willing to pull the plug on what was privately known as Arnie's Albatross, after the pastor who had originally promoted the idea.

Joseph's brothers were starving (see Genesis 43). They wanted to return to Egypt for more food, but their father, Jacob, hesitated on this crucial decision and wasted valuable time hemming and hawing.

❖ *For leaders, tough decisions come with the territory. Make them and move on. You know what needs to be done. More importantly, your people know what needs to be done, and they're waiting for you to do it—now.*

Follow Your Heart

Choose today whom you will serve. Would you prefer the gods your ancestors served beyond the Euphrates? Or will it be the gods of the Amorites in whose land you now live? As for me and my family, we will serve the LORD.   *JOSHUA 24:15*

In the opening credits of Donald Trump's popular television program, *The Apprentice,* the screen flashes a quote from Trump—

"It's not personal. It's business."

The point he's making is that personal feelings shouldn't have a place in the decisions you make regarding business or professional matters.

With respect to Trump for his apparent financial success, I argue that real success in one's professional life comes only when you have invested your passion and your skill.

Joshua's mission was to serve Yahweh, and he was passionate about it. He was committed to the vision that had drawn him into his leadership role. I think Trump would admit to having a passion about what he does as well.

Perhaps you've been criticized for being too passionate, for bringing too much of yourself into the boardroom.

Joshua followed his heart and stood confidently behind his feelings.

❖ *Don't let anyone put out your fire.*

Demonstrate Your Dedication

What is more pleasing to the LORD: your burnt offerings and sacrifices or your obedience to his voice? *1 SAMUEL 15:22*

As I write this, the Winter Olympics are being held in Italy. Watching the figure skaters, I am moved by the incredible skill required to perform at this level. These men and women (boys and girls, in some cases) have dedicated themselves to a standard most of us would choose to avoid.

Even among the upper echelons there are some whose lights shine brighter than the rest. They have something special inside.

The truly great skaters transcend technical expertise and pour their hearts into their performances. They aren't just going through the motions; they're obeying an inner drive that compels them to incredible levels of excellence—and you can see the difference.

Saul followed God's instructions technically, but his heart wasn't in sync.

❖ *What do people see when they watch your performance? Are you skating a technically perfect routine but lacking the personal commitment that makes a real difference?*

Keep On Asking

Keep on asking . . . keep on seeking . . . keep on knocking.   *MATTHEW 7:7*

Allow me to turn a well-known story around for the sake of a lesson.

God loves you and wants to give you good gifts. Yet, despite this desire of God's, Jesus finds it necessary to encourage you to be persistent in your requests.

He tells you to persist in asking, seeking, and knocking.

If God, who *wants* to give us gifts, requires perseverance, how much more persistent should we be when we ask something of someone who cares less for us than God does?

As a leader, you are often in a position to ask people to follow your lead. It can be frustrating when they don't respond to the first request. You seek their support, but it's nowhere to be found.

You knock on their doors, but nobody's home.

The lesson is clear—Jesus encourages us to persistently pursue our desires.

❖ *Don't just sit around waiting for things to happen.*

Smoke Out False Fronts

Everything is pure to those whose hearts are pure.
But nothing is pure to those who are corrupt and
unbelieving, because their minds and consciences
are corrupted.   *TITUS 1:15*

I do a lot of hiking in the Sierra Nevada, especially
around Yosemite National Park, which is home to
some of the oldest giant sequoias in the world.

These great trees have a natural retardant in their
bark, so they can remain standing even if their core
is badly burned by a forest fire. Sometimes a healthy-
looking tree is just a shell of its original self, hollowed
out by fire.

Paul warns against people whose insides have
been gutted by corruption. Like the hollowed-out
sequoias, these people appear to share your values,
but they're incapable of pure motives because their
hearts and minds have atrophied into worthlessness.

Forest rangers keep an eye on these hollowed out
trees because they can easily become diseased and
damage healthy trees nearby.

You'll want to do the same for the people you've
been given to lead.

❖ *Don't be fooled by deceptive exteriors.*

Discern the Times

The captain of the Temple guard and the leading priests . . . were perplexed, wondering where it would all end. Then someone arrived with startling news.   *ACTS 5:24-25*

One of my all-time favorite song lyrics is "You better start swimmin', or you'll sink like a stone" from Bob Dylan's classic folk tune "The Times They Are A-Changin'."

The song speaks of keeping an eye out for changing trends and social currents. Dylan is warning that change is in the wind, and those who ignore this do so at their peril.

The first-century leadership establishment had enjoyed their position for a long time, but the wind was beginning to blow from a new direction and they were confused.

People they had put in prison were suddenly appearing on the streets. These followers of Jesus were turning the world upside down. Traditions were being shattered, and conventions were blown to bits.

Does this sound familiar?

Are you perplexed? I'll bet you know someone who seems to understand what's happening.

❖ *Maybe it's time for some swimming lessons.*

Put God First

Dear children, keep away from anything that might take God's place in your hearts. *1 JOHN 5:21*

In his December 2003 commencement address to undergrads at Biola University, Veggie Tales cocreator Phil Vischer tells the real-life tale of how his incredibly successful animation enterprise was sold to the highest bidder as the result of a brutal legal battle.

Everything he had worked for was gone. The cute characters he and his partner had given birth to and nurtured were now owned by someone else. He wondered why God had taken away a dream that was helping so many kids.

Then it hit him:

"If God gives you a dream and breathes life into it and shows up in it—and it dies, it may be that God wants to know what's more important to you—the dream, or him."

Even if God gave you the mission you're leading, your relationship with him is still more important. No matter what God has given you to do, it must not take God's place in your heart.

❖ *Is there something in your life with a priority higher than God?*

Get Some Rest

On the seventh day God had finished his work of creation, so he rested from all his work.
GENESIS 2:2

Li'l Abner, Dagwood Bumstead, and Beetle Bailey are three of my favorite comic strip characters, because these guys really know how to take a nap. In fact, Li'l Abner—Al Capp's loveable hillbilly—was so good at napping that he earned his living as a professional mattress tester.

Getting enough rest is actually no laughing matter. God was so serious about setting aside time for rest that he "blessed the seventh day and declared it holy, because it was the day when he rested" (Genesis 2:3).

If you are a typical leader, you don't allow yourself enough downtime.

You probably feel that you have a very good reason for pushing beyond your limits. Many overworked leaders believe this is good stewardship of the time God has given them.

Whatever the reason, it doesn't hold water with God, who took the time to provide specific instructions in this regard.

❖ *Follow God's example by building some holy rest into your schedule.*

Spell It Out

When he got home, he took a knife and cut his concubine's body into twelve pieces. Then he sent one piece to each tribe throughout all the territory of Israel. Everyone who saw it said, "Such a horrible crime has not been committed in all the time since Israel left Egypt."   *JUDGES 19:29-30*

We don't know the man's name, but his actions teach us a lesson about "being nice."

The unnamed Levite's concubine had been raped and murdered by the men of Gibeah, and he wanted the entire nation to know about this vile crime. This was not the time to gloss over a problem to protect sensitivities.

He could have sent servants to tell what happened. He could have written a letter to all the tribal leaders. Any number of actions would have been less extreme.

But anything short of what he did would have downplayed the truth of the situation and would thus have been dishonest.

When there's a problem, leaders need to spell it out clearly. State the situation and work toward a solution.

❖ *Are you facing a situation in which you need to be less polite and more truthful?*

Think God's Thoughts

Don't copy the behavior and customs of this world, but let God transform you into a new person by changing the way you think.   *ROMANS 12:2*

There are plenty of excellent business books on the market, but I won't list them because those I find useful might not be appropriate for you and vice versa.

A book on cheese may be more relevant to me than one about fish. You might identify closely with hedgehogs while your partner goes on about purple cows.

The big question is, How well do these books stand against Paul's admonition for us to resist imitating the world's behaviors and customs? Should we ignore their wisdom? Is it even appropriate to weave their lessons into our routines?

The answer lies in the second part of the verse.

God wants your motives to be his motives.

He wants you to think the way he does.

List the key points of your favorite business books, and look for correlations with biblical truth.

❖ *God created purple cows, fish, and hedgehogs. And . . . he's the one who moves your cheese.*

Avoid Senseless Debate

If people are causing divisions among you, give a first and second warning. After that, have nothing more to do with them.   *TITUS 3:10*

Our daughter competed with students from all over the country on her college's varsity debate team.

I teased her about majoring in Argumentation, but parliamentary debate is not about arguing. It's a structured process with limits and rules. Each side presents a case and rebuts the opposing team. At the end of a set length of time, a judge declares the winner.

Some people like to argue just to hear their own voice, and it's these that Paul says aren't worth a third hearing.

You know them. They bring up the same tired arguments every time. They aren't even interested in coming to a conclusion, because doing so would mean having to be quiet and move on.

Paul clearly suggests a solution. Tell them twice that they need to move on, and then cut them off. Have nothing more to do with them.

❖ *You only have so much time. Don't waste it on senseless debate.*

Inform Your Allies

Saul sent this warning to the Kenites: "Move away from where the Amalekites live, or you will die with them. For you showed kindness to all the people of Israel when they came up from Egypt."

1 SAMUEL 15:6

God instructed Saul to wipe out the Amalekite people for something they had done hundreds of years earlier. The Kenites were living nearby, and Saul alerted them to the pending attack so they could move to safety.

Your organization doesn't operate in a vacuum. Decisions you make will affect others, just as the decisions they make have an impact on you.

Before you go public with a major change that has wide-ranging implications, call your allies and give them a heads-up. Let them hear it from you instead of from the news media or the grapevine.

As John Donne, the seventeenth-century poet and clergyman, wrote, "No man is an island." Everyone relies on others.

Do you have something in the works that others should know about before it happens? Set aside time to call them today.

❖ *Make it a practice to keep people in the loop.*

Let Enough Be Enough

Finally Abram said to Lot, "Let's not allow this conflict to come between us or our herdsmen."
GENESIS 13:8

Abram could have pulled rank and simply told Lot which section of land to take, but he exercised exemplary leadership skills by giving Lot first choice of any section he wanted.

Even leaders with the best of intentions fall easily into greediness traps that drive them to extend their influence beyond what they are able to control or maintain. Success in one area causes them to believe they should be successful in another, and another, and another.

This often results in serious damage to the foundational organization that brought them their initial success. Once the foundation begins to crumble, it isn't long before everything comes tumbling down.

Abram knew that no matter which section of land Lot chose, there would still be plenty left for him. He valued his relationship with Lot more than material gain.

❖ *Perhaps you've been looking at other markets or opportunities for expansion. As a leader, it's important for you to know when enough is enough.*

Stay Current

The very next day they began to eat unleavened bread and roasted grain harvested from the land. No manna appeared on the day they first ate from the crops of the land, and it was never seen again. *JOSHUA 5:11-12*

When was the last time you saw a phone booth on a city street? Where hotel lobbies once had rows of pay phones, there's now an empty wall or an Internet kiosk. Kids no longer carry a spare dime to call home.

Does this mean that people have stopped talking to each other by telephone?

Hardly. People still communicate by telephone, but now the phones are wireless and hooked to a belt or a briefcase.

The Israelites had begun a new chapter in their history. They no longer needed the food that had mysteriously appeared each night in the wilderness. The manna had been replaced with something else.

The people were still hungry; they just got their food from a different source.

❖ *Do you have a product or service that's outdated? Perhaps you are asking people to eat manna when they should be looking for a way to bake bread.*

Replace Personnel Thoughtfully

In those days a man will say to his brother, "Since you have a coat, you be our leader! Take charge of this heap of ruins!" *ISAIAH 3:6*

Now there's an interesting job qualification! Things were so bad that people were willing to pick someone to lead on the basis of his wardrobe.

The selection of new leadership is the task most critical to the future of your organization.

Whether the vacancy develops because a good leader moves on or a poor leader is replaced, the opening represents an important milestone.

If you've been blessed with a leadership transition,

+ don't look for someone to fill the shoes of the person who just left. Let the new leader wear his or her own shoes.
+ remember that God created the opening for a reason. Perhaps it will usher in a new style of leadership.
+ be aware that promotion from the inside can often lead to "more of the same."

❖ *This is an opportunity for you to rewrite the future, set a new course, and revitalize the mission. Don't squander it.*

Work Cooperatively

It's not important who does the planting, or who does the watering. What's important is that God makes the seed grow. The one who plants and the one who waters work together with the same purpose. And both will be rewarded for their own hard work.   *1 CORINTHIANS 3:7-8*

Which department most influences your organization's success? Sales? Marketing? Finance? Design? Production? Distribution? Administration? Information Technology?

Could any of them be eliminated? Are any of them indispensable?

Paul faced this issue with the early church. Some people thought Paul was the greatest apostle, while others followed Apollos. Allowing such divisions to continue would have been detrimental to the mission.

As a remedy, Paul reminded the church that the mission was bigger than their personal preferences. They had the same objective—serving Christ—and Paul brought this back into focus.

When you experience turf battles between departments, remind the combatants that they are all working toward the same goal.

❖ *Help your employees keep their eyes on the prize, rather than on their pride.*

Face Forward

I focus on this one thing: Forgetting the past and looking forward to what lies ahead.
PHILIPPIANS 3:13

Here's a time-management tip: Stop thinking about yesterday.

Whether your past was a smashing success or a crashing failure, its only purpose now is to teach you lessons for tomorrow.

Don't waste time reliving or trying to repair the past. Instead, do what the president at my daughter's university encourages students to do: *Carpe Mañana*—"seize tomorrow."

Dr. Bob Brower urges incoming freshman at Point Loma Nazarene University to "do today that which will make a difference tomorrow."

Paul says that he is looking forward to the future. He is giddy with anticipation because he has learned to forget the past and focus on what lies ahead.

Lead your organization toward the future, not the past.

❖ *God gives us a memory of the past so we can learn from it, not live in it.*

Speak Truth to Power

Then the LORD said, "I have seen how stubborn and rebellious these people are. Now leave me alone so my fierce anger can blaze against them. . . ."

But Moses tried to pacify the LORD his God. "O LORD!" he said. "Why are you so angry?"

EXODUS 32:9-11

Yahweh was burning with anger over the golden calf incident and told Moses he had decided to take drastic action.

The ensuing conversation is a great example of the difficult practice known as "speaking truth to power."

Without getting into the theology of the exchange, Moses boldly asserted his case. He presented a reasoned argument, stated some facts about previous commitments, and suggested a course of action.

Moses provided many examples of leadership, but this lesson is about being a graceful follower. The decision belonged to God, but Moses didn't shrink from presenting his case clearly and calmly.

❖ *Moses must have had great faith that his leader would welcome such honesty. Would your people feel the same way about you?*

Be Concise

Too many words make you a fool.   *ECCLESIASTES 5:3*

When Jon Farrar at Tyndale asked me to write this book, he told me the size of the pages would be smaller than usual and that I would need to keep each entry to about 190 words.

The samples I had given him were each about 220 words. I didn't think it was possible to say what was necessary in fewer words, but he was right. Forcing each page down to 190 words helped me to focus on one kernel of truth in each passage. Shorter is definitely better.

Nearly everything we do is too wordy. Sermons are better when they're shorter and more focused.

Marketing brochures with too many words are counterproductive. Job applicants who ramble on rarely get hired. PowerPoint slides with too much information don't help. Just about everything can be said more concisely than what's in the first draft. Avoid over-explaining. Put in what is essential, and don't smother your message with hyperbole.

❖ *Remember to keep it simple.*

Prune with Care

He cuts off every branch of mine that doesn't produce fruit, and he prunes the branches that do bear fruit so they will produce even more.   *JOHN 15:2*

There's a reason why my yard will never be featured in *House Beautiful*. My bushes are scraggly. My lawn has brown splotches, and the few flowers I manage to sustain are always on the verge of dying.

It's not that I don't try. I trim and clip, but I don't really know what I'm doing.

Knowledge in the hands of someone who doesn't have the proper experience can lead to poor decisions and unwanted results.

Jesus implies a certain expertise in this passage. The gardener knew which branches to trim and which to cut off. He carefully followed each twig from beginning to end and made sure the cut was in precisely the right place.

❖ *You may be facing the need for some pruning. Get expert advice and take great care. Consider the consequences. Your goal is to strengthen the vine; make sure you don't kill it off.*

Let Your People Shine

Look, I have specifically chosen Bezalel. . . . I have filled him with the Spirit of God, giving him great wisdom, ability, and expertise in all kinds of crafts. *EXODUS 31:2-3*

I love being around people who are really good at what they do. It gives me great pleasure to watch them because I can tell that they're right in the middle of their sweet spots.

Bono and David Letterman always look as if they wouldn't want to be doing anything else.

Watch Jimmy Carter at a Habitat for Humanity site, and you'll see a guy in his element.

We all know people who are going through the motions of something they aren't very good at. It's where they landed when they got tired of doing what made them happy.

God chose Bezalel to superintend the Tabernacle construction because he was an expert in the field.

❖ *We are all born with a seed of greatness. As a leader, your job is to help people develop whatever will make them shine. Then put their talents to use for the good of the mission.*

Entertain New Ideas

As the Amorites retreated down the road from Beth-horon, the LORD destroyed them with a terrible hailstorm from heaven. . . . The hail killed more of the enemy than the Israelites [had] killed with the sword. *JOSHUA 10:11*

Peter Drucker, the father of modern business consulting, claimed that his greatest strength as a business strategist was the ability to "be ignorant and ask a few questions."

Ignorance allows you to consider solutions that are often rejected by experienced folks who have already decided that something won't work.

Effective problem solving requires you to replace previous solutions with new ideas.

If God had convened a meeting of Joshua's top soldiers and asked them for suggestions on how to defeat the Amorites, I seriously doubt that any of them would have suggested a hailstorm. They were professional military men who would have sought solutions within their scope of expertise.

❖ *If you're looking for unique solutions to vexing issues, look for someone who is ignorant— someone who won't say, "We've always done it this way."*

Don't Overindulge

Don't be greedy, for a greedy person is an idolater, worshiping the things of this world.   COLOSSIANS 3:5

One in three Americans is obese, and two-thirds are overweight because we've forgotten how to say,

"No, thank you. I've had enough."

We have an insatiable appetite for *more*. It's not what we eat that makes us sick, but the sad fact that we don't know when to step away from the table.

Organizations can also display patterns of overindulgence.

Leaders who have lost their ability to step away from the table can develop unhealthy appetites for growth, increased profits, or market dominance, all of which result in serious consequences similar to those brought on by physical obesity.

Paul is not asking you to ignore your desires. On the contrary, God wants to grant the desires of your heart, but he wants you to focus on what's important and learn to control your appetite for more.

Perhaps you've been caught in the greediness trap. Are there projects you've taken on simply because they were on the table?

❖ *Do you need to put your organization on a diet?*

Don't Cheat Your Workers

Listen! Hear the cries of the field workers whom you have cheated of their pay. The wages you held back cry out against you.   *JAMES 5:4*

The immigration issue our country is facing provides a twenty-first-century application of this Scripture, but the leadership lesson goes beyond field-workers.

Consider some of the ways workers get cheated of their pay:

✦ Managers are often too busy to conduct scheduled salary and performance reviews.
✦ Employees are told there's no margin for increased pay, while executive salaries are disproportionately high.
✦ Staff contributions to the health plan are raised so the profit target can be met, allowing for better management bonuses.
✦ A worthy employee is denied a deserved raise because the job market is tight, and he or she can't afford to leave.

Is there anything in your wage and benefit policy that might "cry out against you"?

"Remember, it is sin to know what you ought to do and then not do it" (James 4:17).

❖ *It's all God's money. Be generous with it.*

Provide Clear Instructions

Then God said, "Let there be light." *GENESIS 1:3*

I once managed a team that handled telephone calls from all over the United States and Canada. Since our offices were in California and many customers were on the East Coast, we needed at least one person in the office by 6:00 a.m. to answer calls.

I assumed that my staff would decide for themselves who would take the early shift each day, but I was wrong. There were quite a few mornings when calls went unanswered because no one was in the office to take them.

I called the team together, read Genesis 1:3, and apologized for not stating my desires in clear and concise terms.

"From now on," I told them, "let there be light. I have not been clear enough in stating my expectations, so here they are." After that, I allowed the team to write a schedule, but I required them to run it by me and held them accountable to it, which they appreciated.

❖ *God provides clear and concise instructions. We should do that too.*

Be a Good Steward

Let me pay the full price for the field so I can bury my dead there. *GENESIS 23:13*

There's a common misconception among many leaders that being a good steward of resources requires frequently haggling over purchases to always get the lowest possible price.

Abraham's approach was quite the opposite when he negotiated with Ephron for the purchase of a family burial plot. It was an important piece of property for Abraham, and he showed that he valued the transaction by paying Ephron what the land was worth. Haggling over the price would have indicated that his family's dead were not worth the asking price.

Stewardship involves more than dollars and cents. We're called to be good stewards of our honor and the honor of those with whom we interact.

❖ *Do you have a reputation for always squeezing the lowest price out of suppliers and for being a tough negotiator with partners? If so, take a moment to consider how these folks perceive you. Do they feel honored or beaten when the deal is struck?*

Adjust Your Game Plan

Peter told them, "You know it is against our laws for a Jewish man to enter a Gentile home. . . . But God has shown me that I should no longer think of anyone as impure or unclean." *ACTS 10:28*

National Football League owners gather annually to consider new rules for the league. Most of the changes are minor, but sometimes they initiate sweeping changes, such as the Instant Replay Challenge introduced in 1999.

The goal of the game never changes—but coaches and players adjust to the new rules.

As an observant Jew, Peter played by the rules. He argued when God invited him, in a dream, to eat forbidden food, but the rules had changed, so Peter changed his behavior.

The rules of your game are constantly changing.

Formal letters are now quickie e-mails. Employees move from job to job more often than they used to. Customers make outrageous demands and seem to run the show.

Your success as a leader depends on your ability to adjust to new conditions. Your goal doesn't change, but your game plan must.

❖ *Have the rules changed? Do you need to develop a taste for formerly forbidden food?*

Maximize Your Opportunities

Live wisely among those who are not believers, and make the most of every opportunity.
COLOSSIANS 4:5

The British essayist Adrian Plass suggests in *Jesus: Safe, Tender, Extreme* that Christianity can, at times, be described as a fortress. He writes that Christians sometimes "act in an aggressively defensive manner when we are confronted by ways of thinking that are different from our own."[1]

Maybe that explains the tacit pressure we place on our young people to pursue careers in Christian companies—as if organizations could actually be *saved*.

Paul suggests a different perspective.

Paul doesn't say, "If you *must* work in a secular field. . . ." He simply accepts the reality that we live among people who don't share our beliefs, and he encourages us to live wisely.

Do you work outside the walls of the fort? Are you trying to choose between a Christian company or a secular one?

❖ *Take heart. If you ask God for wisdom, he will help you make the most of every opportunity.*

[1] Adrian Plass, *Jesus: Safe, Tender, Extreme* (Grand Rapids: Zondervan, 2006), 98.

Ignite Your Passion

You are neither hot nor cold. I wish that you were one or the other! But since you are like lukewarm water, neither hot nor cold, I will spit you out of my mouth! *REVELATION 3:15-16*

If two job applicants are equally skilled, I always choose the one who displays more passion for the company's vision and goals.

Passion is the fuel that lifts them above average, into the rarefied air of star performance.

Skilled people are good at what they do, but passionate people are in love with what they do.

The church at Laodicea was competent and rich. They had it all together, and they were very skilled at doing church. Jesus looked past the surface to see that they were miserable, poor, and blind.

Would people on your team describe you as being in love with your mission? Do you wake up every morning giddy with excitement over your to-do list?

Jesus came so you could have an abundant life. He wants you to be as invested in your life as he is.

❖ *Ask him to ignite your passion for leadership.*

Protect Your Product

Gideon made a sacred ephod from the gold. . . .
Soon all the Israelites prostituted themselves by
worshiping it, and it became a trap. *JUDGES 8:27*

The recording industry produces and sells music. For
many years, their product was delivered on records,
tapes, and CDs, but these pieces of plastic were not
the product. They were the tools that carried the
product, which was the music.

These tools became a trap, and the recording
industry lost billions of dollars when consumers no
longer needed them to enjoy the music.

Gideon fashioned an ephod as a tool to help
people worship, but they started to worship the tool,
and it became a trap.

Railroads focused on trains rather than on moving
people from place to place, and they lost ground to
the airline industry in the 1920s. Kodak suffered a
nearly disastrous hit when its leadership was fixated
on film over digital technology in the 1990s.

❖ *Take a moment to think about your product
and the tools you use to deliver it. Don't confuse them. Protect the product, not the tool.*

Play with Patience

This vision is for a future time. . . . If it seems slow in coming, wait patiently, for it will surely take place.   *HABAKKUK 2:3*

When working with leaders, I often ask whether they prefer to play checkers or chess.

In checkers, the object of each move is to jump as many of your opponent's pieces as possible. A game of checkers can be over in less than a minute.

Chess requires intense concentration and extreme patience. Great chess players plot out entire games in their heads before making a single move. The time between moves is often monitored by a stop clock, and games can last for days.

God is the ultimate chess player.

He gave Habakkuk a vision of the future, with the proviso that the realization of the vision was a long way off.

❖ *How patient are you? Are you more likely to run the board and jump every piece, or can you wait patiently until all the parts of your plan fall into place?*

Back Your Players

"O Sovereign LORD," I said, "I can't speak for you! I'm too young!" The LORD replied, "Don't say, 'I'm too young.' . . . Don't be afraid . . . for I will be with you." *JEREMIAH 1:6-8*

The boss was sending Eric, the youngest member of their executive team, on a difficult assignment. To ensure that folks in the field would take him seriously, the boss took time to call each of the managers Eric would be visiting. She encouraged them to treat the new guy with respect.

At each stop along the way, Eric was met with enthusiasm and support because his boss was behind him.

It's tough for young leaders to earn respect from the old guard, so do what you can to smooth the path for them. Let others know the newbies have your support. And for goodness' sake, don't send them on a trip that no one else wants to make!

❖ *God's task for Jeremiah was extremely important. Jeremiah could step out with confidence because he knew that God was with him.*

Choose Names Carefully

What's more, I am changing your name. It will
no longer be Abram. Instead, you will be called
Abraham.   *GENESIS 17:5*

With apologies to Shakespeare, I don't think my wife
would appreciate receiving a dozen artichokes for
Valentine's Day—even if they did smell like roses.

A rose by any other name would not be a rose.

Names are symbols that speak volumes about a
product or the type of service you can expect from a
particular organization.

One of the first tasks God gave Adam was to name
the animals. When God was ready to initiate a new
chapter in Abram's life, he marked the occasion by
changing his name. This was no small thing.

It is easy to think that names are less important
than quality products, good service, and high ideals,
but history is littered with decent ideas that never
went anywhere because people couldn't (or wouldn't)
get past their names.

The Chevy Nova was wildly popular in the United
States, but sales stalled in Latin America because the
name translates literally as "No Go," which is hardly
a good name for a car. I'm sure there are other examples, but who can remember them?

❖ *The Master of the Universe sees the impor-*
tance of names. You should too.

Don't Be Greedy

I have more than enough.   *GENESIS 33:11*

I may lose you on this one, and if I do, thanks for sticking around this long.

There is a tragic tendency among many people in leadership positions to measure success by the amount of stuff they accumulate over time.

Being *first* has taken precedence over being *excellent*.

Having *enough* has been replaced by *wanting more.*

There is nothing intrinsically improper about desiring more, but the levels to which we take this have exacted a horrible toll from families, faith, and personal health.

Perhaps you are at a crossroads on this issue right now. Take heart in realizing that you are not alone. There is a strong current of disillusionment among people who have been taught to always stay one step ahead.

I'll bet that it wouldn't take too long for you to find a kindred spirit if you just started adding this simple phrase to your conversation with friends: "I'm beginning to think I have more than enough."

❖ *You may be amazed at the reaction you get.*

Question Conventional Wisdom

The entire city turned out to hear them preach the word of the Lord. But when some of the Jews saw the crowds, they were jealous; so they slandered Paul and argued against whatever he said.

ACTS 13:44-45

Here's some encouragement: If the establishment in your industry or circle of influence is criticizing your success, you are probably doing something right—so slap on a smile and keep it up.

You're in good company if conventional wisdom finds your ideas foolish.

✦ Christopher Columbus: "The world isn't flat."
✦ Martin Luther King Jr.: "I have a dream."
✦ Ronald Reagan: "Tear down this wall."
✦ Jesus the Nazarene: "Lose your life to gain it."

With only a slight bit of sarcasm, I suggest that you should be the most concerned when everyone agrees with you. If that's the case, you're probably not being very effective.

Paul never ran from criticism, although his friends often begged him to avoid it. Thankfully, he didn't listen to them.

New ideas are uncomfortable. Success breeds jealousy.

❖ *Are you feeling the heat? That's awesome. Pour it on.*

Prepare for Mission-Critical Events

Then Jesus was led by the Spirit into the wilderness. *MATTHEW 4:1*

Trade shows are a lot of work. As an exhibitor, our company begins to plan nearly a year in advance, and activity increases to a frenzy in the weeks right before showtime. I often arrive at a convention with a bad cold or fever because I am so run-down from all the preparations.

Every organization has mission-critical events— trade shows, annual sales, Easter services, donor banquets. As a leader, it's your job to make sure your people have adequate time to prepare them- selves—mentally and physically—for the rigors of these events.

Jesus was led into the wilderness to fast and pray in the days just before his ministry began. He resisted temptation during this time and set us the good example of taking time to focus our thoughts and energies before any mission-critical activity.

❖ *Resist the temptation to head into an impor- tant time with less than a full measure of rest.*

Be Culturally Savvy

When Pharaoh . . . asks you about your occupation, you must tell him, "We . . . have raised livestock all our lives, as our ancestors have always done." When you tell him this, he will let you live here in . . . Goshen, for the Egyptians despise shepherds.   *GENESIS 46:33-34*

A friend of mine is an executive at a large firm in the United States. A few years back, his company was purchased by an organization headquartered in Europe, and his life became an absolute nightmare.

The new owners didn't understand American work culture. They tried to change everything—vacations, sick pay, family leave, health benefits, labor relations—and the result was a dramatic drop in productivity for their newly acquired division.

The new policies weren't wrong—they were just different and were implemented in a way that seemed to dishonor American sensitivities.

In Genesis, Joseph understood the potential disasters of blending two cultures, so he took steps to mitigate their differences.

❖ *If you're called upon to lead a cultural merger of multiple organizations, do whatever you can to preserve the unique qualities that gave each team its original success.*

Treasure Simplicity

My message and my preaching were very plain.
Rather than using clever and persuasive speeches,
I relied only on the power of the Holy Spirit.
1 CORINTHIANS 2:4

"Four score and seven years ago our fathers brought
forth, upon this continent, a new nation."

President Abraham Lincoln wrote and delivered
his Gettysburg Address in November 1863. Lincoln
reportedly wrote this speech on the train between
Washington and Gettysburg.

As presidential speeches go, it's one of the shortest,
coming in at less than three hundred words. Maybe
that's why it has stood the test of time.

Paul shares a valuable lesson that Lincoln must
have known:

There is power in simplicity.

When your message is true—as Paul's was—you
don't need to hide behind superlatives and hype. In
fact, the hoopla often detracts from the focus of what
you're trying to accomplish.

❖ *I'm not arguing for poorly written or inane
communication (neither Paul nor Lincoln
insulted their readers' intelligence), but take a
look at your letters, news releases, and marketing copy. Do you need a superlative filter?*

Keep Your Promises

Let us hold tightly without wavering to the hope we affirm, for God can be trusted to keep his promise.   *HEBREWS 10:23*

God does what he says he will do.

This commitment to commitment is a very attractive leadership trait. The degree to which you follow through on your promises will have a profound effect on your success as a leader.

Consider the longevity of a little book named *Horton Hatches the Egg*, which was written in 1940 by Theodor "Dr. Seuss" Geisel. It's the story of an elephant who is tricked into sitting on the egg of an irresponsible bird. The bird disappears, but Horton refuses to give up his post on the nest because

"I meant what I said and I said what I meant, an elephant's faithful, 100 percent."

Horton remains a favorite of children and parents because the idea of keeping one's promises appeals to our deepest longings. We want to trust people, and we'll cling to anyone who is worthy of our hope.

❖ *Are you faithful, 100 percent?*

Offer a Plan

The people were all shouting, some one thing and some another. Everything was in confusion. In fact, most of them didn't even know why they were there. *ACTS 19:32*

The people of Ephesus were rioting, and they didn't even know why.

A silversmith named Demetrius had taken issue with Paul for preaching that there was only one true God. Demetrius sold handmade silver gods. He provoked a group of fellow craftsmen, whose anger boiled at the thought of losing their business to this new "one God" idea.

Their passion spilled into the streets, and as Luke writes, "soon the whole city was filled with confusion" (Acts 19:29).

The same scenario occurs today. It seldom manifests as a riot, but people will rally behind one idea or another despite knowing little about it. We play "follow the leader," but we don't know where the leader is going.

Here's the good news: Confused people are eager to follow someone with a plan.

❖ *Are you standing in the midst of a confused crowd? Try raising a banner that says, "Follow me—I have a plan." You'll be amazed at what happens.*

Don't Exploit People

You must not exploit a widow. . . . If you exploit
them in any way . . . I will certainly hear their cry.
My anger will blaze against you.   EXODUS 22:22-24

You learn that a supplier has had a run of bad
luck and is hurting for cash to meet short-term
obligations.

Do you . . .
  Take advantage of the supplier's vulnerability and
     demand that he "sharpen his pencil" before you
     finalize an order you already intended to place?
Or do you . . .
  Acknowledge the supplier's dilemma and pay full
     price as a way of helping him get back on his
     feet?

If the business turns around, you will have a dedicated supplier who bends over backward for you. If it
doesn't, you haven't paid any more than you intended
to pay in the first place, and you've honored someone
by being gracious to them during a difficult time.

❖ *Taking advantage of someone's misfortune is
not good stewardship.*

Spice It Up

God made two great lights. . . . He also made the stars.   *GENESIS 1:16*

Visit any restaurant where the food doesn't come in a bag, and you'll see some sort of garnish on the side of the plate—orange slices, parsley sprigs, cherry peppers, or even little orchid blossoms. No one ever eats the stuff, but the plate would look unfinished without a garnish.

Surely the sun and moon would have been enough for God to create. One lit up the daytime sky, and the other governed the night, but God understood the need for garnish.

Imagine how bare the evening sky would seem without stars. Also, just as parsley is useful in cleansing your breath or settling your stomach, stars serve a useful purpose for navigation (and childhood wishes).

❖ *When you're designing a new product or service, take a step back and look beyond the utilitarian basics. Is there a garnish that would add value to an otherwise mundane presentation?*

Cultivate a Pleasing Aroma

This is a burnt offering to the LORD; it is a pleasing aroma. *EXODUS 29:18*

Brain scientists know that smells are processed by a section of the brain that is directly linked to our emotions. The other four senses are processed through our conscious minds, but aromas go straight to our feelings.

You can program your brain's reaction to sights, sounds, touch, and taste, but smells cause immediate, involuntary chemical reactions, such as the joy a mom feels when she picks up her baby's blankie and draws in a deep breath.

How does your organization smell?

What "aroma" do you present to people on the outside?

What immediate and uncontrollable reaction do people experience when they come into contact with your staff?

What about your personal scent? This has nothing to do with perfume or aftershave. It's all about how others *feel* when they're around you.

Do they fill their lungs with a deep, satisfying breath? Do they hold their noses and make for the nearest exit?

❖ *People seldom remember what you tell them, but they always recall how you made them feel.*

Take a Deep Breath

David would play the harp. Then Saul would feel better, and the tormenting spirit would go away.
1 SAMUEL 16:23

On occasion, leadership duties can be overwhelming. I'm sure you've been there. You may be there right now.

Most people in leadership positions are good problem solvers. A typical reaction to overload is to push harder, but that's not always the best course of action.

Sometimes it helps to step aside and enjoy some harp music for a few minutes.

What works for you? Is it a CD with classical music? What about 1960s rock and roll? Do you walk around the block to clear your head? Perhaps you call an old friend or walk to the bookshelf and look closely at pictures of your family on vacation last year.

King Saul was troubled for a variety of reasons, not the least of which was his disobedient nature. He was the most powerful man in Israel, yet he found comfort in something as simple as harp music played by a shepherd from Bethlehem.

❖ *It's okay to draw a deep breath now and then.*

Agree to Disagree

Barnabas . . . wanted to take along John Mark. But Paul disagreed strongly. . . . Their disagreement was so sharp that they separated. Barnabas took John Mark with him and sailed for Cyprus.
ACTS 15:37-39

I love the way God includes the dirty laundry in his book.

Paul and Barnabas had a heated disagreement over John Mark, a young man who had left the ministry and then returned. The result was a temporary separation, with Paul and Barnabas going in different directions.

Paul and Barnabas didn't see the need to negotiate a middle-ground resolution. Each was convinced that his own opinion was correct, and there's no evidence that God was upset with either decision. Both were subsequently blessed with successful ministries.

Leadership teams often waste valuable time trying to hammer out compromises that yield mediocre results.

Mutual and genuine respect is obligatory for anyone on a leadership team, but progress should never be held hostage by a demand for consensus.

❖ *God made us all different. We won't always march to the same drum.*

Discard Bad Apples

Get rid of the old "yeast" by removing this wicked person from among you. Then you will be like a fresh batch of dough made without yeast, which is what you really are.   *1 CORINTHIANS 5:7*

There's a farmers' market in our town, and I go crazy there each summer buying way too much fruit at one time. Before we can eat it all, one piece will develop a bit of decay, and if I don't get the offending fruit out of the basket right away, the entire bunch goes bad overnight.

With apologies to Michael Jackson, who had a hit song to the contrary, one bad apple *can* spoil the whole bunch.

Paul warns against people who plant seeds of discontent. He compares them to a bit of yeast that spreads quickly through a batch of dough by multiplying itself.

A tiny speck of yeast can ruin a batch of unleavened bread, and a bad apple can turn the whole basket to mush. One person with a bad attitude can spell big trouble for your team.

❖ *Paul's advice is clear. Read the verse again.*

Avoid a Leadership Void

In those days Israel had no king; all the people did whatever seemed right in their own eyes.
JUDGES 17:6

The orchestra was performing outside. In the middle of a tune, a gust of wind caught the conductor's music and blew it onto the grass.

As he reached down to retrieve his music, his musicians were momentarily without a leader. It sounded okay for a few moments, but without his consistent direction, some played a bit faster and others a bit slower.

They were all doing what they *thought* was right.

With no leader, the Israelites did what they thought was right. They weren't trying to do wrong; they just didn't have anyone to direct them.

Leadership voids can happen even with someone standing in a leadership position. People follow a leader who is decisive, focused, productive, and always looking to the future.

Perhaps your team has been unfocused lately, each doing what he or she thinks is right, all of them differently.

❖ *Are you leading or reaching down to retrieve your music?*

Delegate Appropriate Authority

King Artaxerxes had given a copy of the following letter to Ezra: . . . "From Artaxerxes, the king of kings, to Ezra the priest, the teacher of the law of the God of heaven." *EZRA 7:11-12*

My assignment was to help a company reorganize a department that was hemorrhaging money. One of my first steps was to overhaul a poorly managed out-of-state office.

Previous attempts to do so had failed because the people sent to fix things were considered junior level and couldn't demand change. They were easy to ignore because they lacked the proper authority.

I asked for, and received, a personal letter from the CEO that spelled out my assignment and instructed the manager to cooperate fully with my requests. It worked.

Ezra had a job to do. Artaxerxes made sure he could do it by officially announcing his support of the project. The king made sure everyone knew that Ezra was working on his behalf.

❖ *When you give someone a sensitive assignment, take the time to add your formal stamp of approval. Leave no doubt that he or she has your blessing and your authority.*

Limit Meaningless Chatter

Then Job spoke again: "You people really know everything, don't you? . . . Well, I know a few things myself." *JOB 12:1-3*

Every now and then, the media runs a story about a public figure who puts aside his or her facade and responds to someone who has been haranguing him or her. It's often a politician, and the dialogue tends to be rather crude, but the lesson is valuable.

Job's friends were downright annoying. None of their ideas were helpful. Heeding their advice would have caused Job to sin, and he knew it. There was nothing to be gained by listening to them any longer.

Job did what more leaders should do: He told them to sit down and be quiet.

There are only so many minutes in a day; filling them with twaddle wastes precious time.

Listening to different opinions is valuable. Paying attention to new ideas keeps you on your toes. Make sure that you have enough time for what is important by limiting the amount of garbage you will listen to.

❖ *Is there someone who wastes your time?*

Be a Good Servant

You know that the rulers in this world lord it over their people, and officials flaunt their authority over those under them. But among you it will be different. Whoever wants to be a leader among you must be your servant, and whoever wants to be first among you must become your slave.

MATTHEW 20:25-27

I love the line in the middle of this passage:

"Among you it will be different."

You are called to be a different type of leader.

Good servants anticipate the needs of those they serve. They don't wait to be asked, but look ahead for ways they can help others.

Slaves can't demand their own way. They humbly do whatever is needed to get the job done.

"Among you it will be different."

❖ *How is your leadership style different?*

Challenge Authority Respectfully

Everyone must submit to governing authorities. For all authority comes from God, and those in positions of authority have been placed there by God. So anyone who rebels against authority is rebelling against what God has instituted. *ROMANS 13:1-2*

When you work for someone, he or she sets the agenda. Your job is to do what you're trained to do, within the standards and guidelines set by the person who signs your paycheck.

What if they're wrong? What if they're making a mistake?

Learn to effect change while respecting the standards you are trying to alter.

If policy dictates that you color inside the lines, request specific permission to go outside the lines. Be clear about why you think it's a good idea and what you hope to accomplish. Suggest a way to measure the results of your new idea. Show respect by providing regular updates on your nonstandard activities.

Paul may have been thinking of how Jesus handled the religious establishment of his day. He respected their position as Jewish leaders, while always suggesting a better way to do things.

❖ *Raise your hand and say, "May I have your permission to break the rules?"*

Pay Your Taxes

"Well, then," Jesus said, "give to Caesar what belongs to Caesar, and give to God what belongs to God." *MARK 12:17*

The church I attend enjoys the property-tax exemption that is extended to houses of worship. As long as we avoid profit-making enterprises, we don't pay the tax.

An attorney joined our board and suggested that our occasional book table and various other activities violated the exemption. He suggested we designate a small area as nonexempt and pay a minimum tax on it.

It saddened me to learn of quite a few local churches that were willing to ignore the law rather than, as Jesus instructed, "give to Caesar" what was legally due.

Most see the law as unfair, and even silly, but Scripture is quite clear on our responsibility to obey it, or work to change it *while obeying it.*

How are you doing in this area? Are you obeying the law in your hiring? Taxes? Computer software and copyright laws?

❖ *In this case, it's not a case of wondering what would Jesus do. We have a clear example of what Jesus did.*

Be Visible

And the LORD did not remove the pillar of cloud or pillar of fire from its place in front of the people. *EXODUS 13:22*

One of your tasks as a leader is to maintain a sense of security for your people. One way you can do this is to let them see you in the building.

If you're never in the office, they will start to wonder if you even know what's going on.

If your door is always closed, they'll suspect you are hiding from something.

Being out where folks can see you will do wonders for people's perception that you are actually in charge.

The Hebrews could look up at any time and see the sign of God's presence. There was no doubt that he was involved in the process of getting them to the Promised Land.

An approach that works for some people is called MBWA—Management by Walking Around. The physical presence of the person in charge can do wonders for motivation and morale.

❖ *How would your people rate your involvement in the process?*

Ask for Success

Please give me success today.　　*GENESIS 24:12*

Let's be straight as an arrow about this:
   It is okay to succeed at something.
   It is okay to want success.
   It is okay to do what needs to be done to achieve
        success.

The key to making it work in a God-honoring way is to have the right motives. Abraham's servant was given a task to complete, and he wanted to please his master, so he asked God to grant him success.

   Your definition of success may need to be altered. Is "winning the race" your goal, or is achieving a personal best the real measure of success?

❖ *As a leader, you should desire success, not for what it can do for you, but for how you can use it to bless others.*

Be Careful What You Ask For

Then God said . . . and that is what
happened.   *GENESIS 1:6-7*

The president of a rapidly growing company was
concerned with a perception that members of his
executive team spent more time on the road than
with their families. At a staff meeting attended by the
accounting manager, he suggested that no one should
leave town more than once a month.

The president intended this comment as a guide-
line rather than an edict, but the accounting manager
took his words at face value (as she should have
done) and refused to honor expense vouchers for
excessive travel until another meeting was held to
explain what the boss really meant.

Leaders are in a position to bring about change
just by stating a desire for something. Be careful of
what you say outside the protection of your office.
Plenty of shocked CEOs have learned that an off-
hand comment made in an elevator has become
woven into the fabric of their companies' new policy
manuals.

❖ *Be careful what you ask for—people really
are listening.*

Discover Your Strengths

I am the LORD your God . . . and I have put my
words in your mouth and hidden you safely in my
hand. I stretched out the sky like a canopy and laid
the foundations of the earth. I am the one who says
to Israel, "You are my people!"   *ISAIAH 51:15-16*

I am convinced that God has a unique plan for your
life. God, who created the complexity of everything
you see, breathed his Spirit into you.

You were created with a special skill set that fits
perfectly into his big picture for the universe.

Have you taken time to discover what those skills
are? Do you know what you're good at?

We often concentrate on our faults, to the detri-
ment of our strengths.

I highly recommend that you read *Now, Discover
Your Strengths* by Marcus Buckingham and Donald
O. Clifton. This book will help you identify your
God-given skills and show you how to develop them
into strengths.

❖ *Be encouraged. God made you the way you
are.*

Use a Safety Net

The LORD will go ahead of you; yes, the God of Israel will protect you from behind.   *ISAIAH 52:12*

"Ladies and gentlemen, please direct your attention to the center ring, where the Amazing Velendas will perform their high-wire magic. Notice that there is no safety net."

Why do some people insist on balancing twenty feet above the ground without a net? Having a net doesn't make the balancing act any less spectacular. Their performance would be even more amazing if they knew there was something to catch them if they fell.

Leading an organization puts you in precarious positions. You're the one who floats the crazy new idea. You're the one who has to explain why it didn't quite work as planned.

All eyes are on you.

Isaiah had confidence because he knew the Lord was covering his back. He could move out boldly, knowing there was a net beneath him if he stumbled.

Do you have a net? Do you have a network of people who will support you when things don't go as planned?

❖ *You needn't walk the tightrope alone.*

Set High Standards

Select only strong, healthy, and good-looking young men," he said. "Make sure they are well versed in every branch of learning . . . and are suited to serve in the royal palace. *DANIEL 1:4*

My friend Brent, an executive-placement specialist, has helped some of the biggest companies in the world fill their most critical job openings. I once worked with him on a search committee and learned an important lesson about the hiring process:

You'll never regret setting high standards.

Nebuchadnezzar was recruiting new palace staff. He had high standards, and even after choosing some candidates, he fed and groomed them for three years before making his final choices.

You don't have the luxury of a three-year search, but the lesson remains the same: Hire the best candidates money can buy.

Don't scrimp on your salary offer. If they refuse, you've lost. If they accept, you're being unfair if the offer could have been higher.

Employees are more valuable than equipment, and companies rarely buy the cheapest machine for a critical job.

❖ *Isn't the quality of your team worth every penny?*

Set an Example

Judge fairly, and show mercy and kindness to one another. Do not oppress widows, orphans, foreigners, and the poor. And do not scheme against each other.   *ZECHARIAH 7:9-10*

I have been pondering this passage for nearly twenty-four hours. I am trying to find a relevant lesson, because you deserve more than my simply saying, "Read this and do what it says."

And here's what I have: You must become an example.

Become a shining light of genuine fairness, mercy, and kindness to the world.

Speak and act against the mistreatment of widows (single moms), parentless kids, alien workers (legal and illegal), and those whose personal economies are in worse shape than your own.

Take a leadership role in getting along with fellow followers of Jesus; work together for everyone's good.

Zechariah reminds Israel that their "ancestors refused to listen to this message" (7:11), which is why the Lord was so angry with them.

❖ *It can start with you. It **must** start with you. Who else will do it?*

Prepare Your People

God blesses you when people mock you. . . . Be happy about it! Be very glad! For a great reward awaits you in heaven. *MATTHEW 5:11-12*

Command Headquarters—Bahrain, Saudi Arabia—February 1991

"Well, boys, this is it. We'll get our battle orders within the next six hours, and then it's over the line into enemy territory. I'm going to give it to you straight—this is not going to be a cakewalk. We are in for the battle of our lives. But that's what we've trained for. You men are part of the best fighting army in history. Our gear is better, our training is better, and we are better. Now, let's get ready to give 'em what they came for."

Good leaders prepare their people for tough times by telling them the truth.

Jesus warned his followers about the difficulties that lay ahead, and he gave them hope for the future by painting a picture of what was waiting at the end.

❖ *Have you shared both the hard reality of the mission and the joy of the reward with your team?*

Examine Your Traditions

So the Pharisees and teachers of religious law asked him, "Why don't your disciples follow our age-old tradition? They eat without first performing the hand-washing ceremony." *MARK 7:5*

There's an old story about a cage full of monkeys who are blasted with ice water every time one of them reaches for a banana. The monkeys are replaced one by one, and the cold-water spray eventually stops, but the monkeys still refuse to reach for the fruit.

If monkeys could talk, they couldn't tell you *why* the bananas were off-limits, but they would know that reaching for one was something you just didn't do.

The Pharisees were not bad guys. They were following the rules—the way they'd always done it—but they had lost track of the reasons behind their traditions and had gotten their priorities out of whack.

Jesus didn't criticize the Pharisees for following the rules, but for making the rules their highest goal. They got into trouble because the way they'd always done it had become their priority.

❖ *What ways you've always done it have become stuck-in-the-mud traditions? Is it time for a change?*

Tell Your Own Story

But others in the crowd ridiculed them, saying, "They're just drunk, that's all!" Then Peter stepped forward with the eleven other apostles and shouted to the crowd.   *ACTS 2:13-14*

The company had launched a new concept that would revolutionize business models in a very conservative industry. The new ideas were solid and promised great value to those who would adopt them.

The overwhelming buzz was negative. Trade journals panned the ideas, and loyal customers spoke openly against them.

Nearly all the criticism was unfounded.

The new ideas were solid, but the company had decided to use a soft launch. They never stepped up to tell their side of the story.

Human nature will always assume the worst. In an information vacuum, people will invent a negative scenario. You may have the best intentions and the most solid plan, but if you don't tell your own story, others will make one up for you.

The apostles were launching a controversial new idea. Until Peter stepped up to explain what was happening, the buzz was overwhelmingly negative.

❖ *Tell your own story.*

Share Your Joys

Two people are better off than one, for they can help each other succeed. . . . Three are even better, for a triple-braided cord is not easily broken.

ECCLESIASTES 4:9, 12

This scripture is often used to encourage people to find someone with whom they can share accountability. Here is another application that you may not have considered:

Success is a lot more enjoyable when you share it with someone.

The author of Ecclesiastes had observed a person who "works hard to gain as much wealth as he can" only to realize that he's been "giving up so much pleasure" by working alone (4:8).

Are there people in your life with whom you can share the fruit of your labor? Are you working too hard to enjoy the harvest of your efforts? What good is all the sweat, if all you do at the end is turn it over to someone else?

❖ *To paraphrase the book of Ecclesiastes, God gave you a life to enjoy, and you can only do that while you're alive, so start enjoying it now.*

Live Abundantly

Jacob worked seven years to pay for Rachel. But his love for her was so strong that it seemed to him but a few days.   *GENESIS 29:20*

There is tremendous wisdom in the saying, "Love what you do; do what you love."

God did not intend for our work to be a drag. He made us each unique and gave us a purpose so that we could experience life in all its fullness, as Jesus promised (see John 10:10).

The secret is to live the life God intended for you, using the talents he gave you and seeking his purpose. When you finally stop trying to fit into a box you've made for yourself and begin to focus on God's plan for you, your fatigue and lousy attitude will begin to fade away.

Jacob worked seven years for Laban in exchange for Rachel's hand. I'm sure he was physically tired at the end of each day, but his attitude didn't suffer because he had a purpose. Jacob had his eye on the prize, and the days flew by.

❖ *Are you living the abundant life? Do you need to make some changes?*

Pay the Price

Then Samuel said to all the people of Israel, "If you are really serious about wanting to return to the LORD . . ." *1 SAMUEL 7:3*

An accomplished pianist was playing one day for a friend, who remarked, "I would give anything to play the piano like that."

The musician answered, "No, you wouldn't." He described the sacrifices of time, relationships, and opportunities he had paid to become the virtuoso he was.

Success had come at a great cost, which he gladly paid because he was serious about being excellent in his chosen field.

When the people of Israel told Samuel what they wanted, he judged their sincerity by the price they were willing to pay.

❖ *Being a leader does not come without a price tag. Have you considered the cost? Are you serious about wanting to succeed?*

Do What You Do Best

God blessed them, saying, "Be fruitful and multiply. Let the fish fill the seas." GENESIS 1:22

Here is another example in which God gave specific instructions regarding a desired outcome. But, unlike other instances in which he provided a detailed, step-by-step manual for proper conduct, he simply told the fish to do what they did best.

God is aware of what fish are capable of doing, and he knows they will fulfill their responsibilities without direct supervision.

Wouldn't it be great if the people on your team were as dependable as fish?

The secret could lie in your describing your desired final outcome and then stepping back to let them do what they do best. Everyone on your team has a God-given skill.

❖ *If you know what your team members were created to do, and you encourage them to be all God wants them to be, you'll have oceans of "fish" to harvest.*

Add Some Margin

You have six days each week for your ordinary work, but on the seventh day you must stop working, even during the seasons of plowing and harvest. *EXODUS 34:21*

Richard Swenson opens his book *Margin* with this observation:

> The conditions of modern-day living devour margin. . . . [Living without margin] is being thirty minutes late to the doctor's office because you were twenty minutes late getting out of the hairdresser's because you were ten minutes late dropping off the children at school.
>
> Margin, on the other hand, is having breath left at the top of the staircase, money left at the end of the month, and sanity left at the end of [the day].[1]

Maybe you'd love to take a day to relax, but you're afraid that work would just pile up.

If there is more to do than you have time for, perhaps you should evaluate what you're doing to see if it's all really necessary.

❖ *Wouldn't it be wonderful to read this page next year and smile because you've finally been able to tackle the beast of busyness and add some margin into your life?*

1 Richard A. Swenson, *Margin: Restoring Emotional, Physical, Financial, and Time Reserves to Overloaded Lives* (Colorado Springs: NavPress, 1992), 13.

Think Grand Thoughts

"My thoughts are nothing like your thoughts," says the LORD. "And my ways are far beyond anything you could imagine." *ISAIAH 55:8*

Here's another of God's leadership attributes we can imitate: He encourages us to dream big dreams and think grand thoughts.

God described his new plan for salvation to Isaiah. He had already said that he was going to do something new, and here he issued a challenge: "Go ahead and dream. I want you to stretch your mind. I'm not concerned, because there's no way you are going to come up with anything bigger or grander or more spectacular than I have."

God plants seeds of vision in you; he wants you to take your skills as far as they will go. Don't hold back. God takes pleasure in watching his children do what he created them to do.

Go for it.

While you're at it, issue the same challenge to the people who report to you. Give them the freedom to think beyond the horizon.

❖ *Learn to say, "Here's my idea. How can we make it better?"*

Do What Is Right

The Lord has told you what is good, and this is what he requires of you: to do what is right, to love mercy, and to walk humbly with your God.
MICAH 6:8

Far too many followers of Jesus draw a very thick line between their personal walk with God and their business practices.

In the name of good stewardship, they pay their employees less than they should. They talk about tithing, while they pay less tax than they owe. They habitually squeeze suppliers and merchants for unreasonable discounts.

In Micah 6:10-12, God lists some sinful practices that sound like the standard "unwritten" policy for some organizations.

God is very clear about his displeasure with this and says, "I will bring you to ruin for all your sins" (Micah 6:13).

❖ *God doesn't separate personal from public, or spiritual from professional. Neither should you.*

Find a Quiet Place

The apostles returned to Jesus from their ministry tour and told him all they had done and taught. Then Jesus said, "Let's go off by ourselves to a quiet place and rest awhile." *MARK 6:30-31*

I can't think of a stronger endorsement for the value of corporate retreats than Jesus' taking his team to a quiet place to rest awhile.

Jesus knew his time was limited, and he knew the tremendous task facing his disciples. Yet he suggested that they go on a retreat.

Your calendar is packed from now until the pages run out. Everyone on the team is busy. There is no way you can possibly schedule a retreat.

I've heard all the excuses and made a few of them myself. None of the reasons for avoiding a retreat stand up to Jesus' example.

Are you serious about asking, "What would Jesus do?"

❖ *Get out your calendar, call your lead team together, and schedule a time to find a quiet place to rest awhile.*

Pray for More Workers

The harvest is great, but the workers are few. So pray to the Lord who is in charge of the harvest; ask him to send more workers into his fields.

LUKE 10:2

How many hours a week are you expected to work? Fifty hours? Sixty? Seventy?

Many organizations have reduced staff levels. Those who remain are expected to pick up excess work, while maintaining a commitment to growth. The work force is asked to do much more with far less—a practice I think Jesus would discourage.

Jesus acknowledged that there was more work than his team could handle. Instead of mandating better time-management skills or trading family time for overtime, he told them to pray for more help so the extra work could be accomplished.

People shouldn't be asked to do more than they can physically, mentally, or emotionally handle. If the work exceeds your staffing ability, you need to reduce expectations to a level your people can handle.

❖ *If your goals are that important, hire enough people to get the job done.*

Practice the Future

[God] has planted eternity in the human heart, but even so, people cannot see the whole scope of God's work from beginning to end.
ECCLESIASTES 3:11

My cat does not think about what will happen when his food bowl is empty. He gets up every morning and eats. If there's nothing in the bowl, he bugs me until I fill it. God has not "planted eternity" in his heart.

Being ignorant of the future and taking things only as they come along—like my cat—is foolhardy. On the flip side, forecasting the future is only making an educated guess concerning what *might* happen at a given point.

How can you prepare for an uncertain future?

I encourage leaders to "practice the future" by playing "what if" games:

+ *What if* our largest supplier shuts down?
+ *What if* we grow by 30 percent in the next five years?
+ *What if* the government bans our products or services?

❖ *Perhaps God gives us a glimpse of the future so we are compelled to trust him with the details we're not allowed to see.*

Get Fresh Intelligence

Gideon took Purah and went down to the edge of the enemy camp. The armies of Midian . . . [were] like a swarm of locusts. Their camels were like grains of sand on the seashore.   *JUDGES 7:11-12*

Gideon had every right to be concerned about his pending battle against the Midianite army. From a distant perspective, these guys were going to be tough opponents.

There were three hundred Israelites against an army described as "too many to count" (Judges 7:12).

But wait—Gideon overheard two of the enemy soldiers talking, and they were terrified. They had dreams about being beaten by Gideon and were convinced of their own demise.

Good intelligence is critically important. When you're faced with a tough decision, get all the facts. Overestimating your opponent's abilities is just as detrimental as overestimating your own. Having the latest intelligence can give you tremendous confidence.

❖ *How fresh is your information?*

Dare to Dream On

"Here comes the dreamer!" they said. "Come on, let's kill him and throw him into one of these cisterns." *GENESIS 37:19-20*

This pivotal moment in Joseph's life highlights the perpetual struggle between those who see the need for change (the dreamers) and those who are heavily invested in the past (the settlers).

Settlers always seem to be in charge. By their nature, they stick around and establish roots. When dreamers come along and suggest there might be something outside the walls, they are thrown into cisterns.

Dreamers always pay a price, but in exchange for the hazards, they are rewarded with the glory of a new idea before it's dented and bent by settlers who squeeze it into their visions of the past.

My friend Howard Potratz says there's no better feeling than the one that lasts for about ten seconds between the time you float out a brand-new idea and the time someone tells you it will never work.

❖ *He's right, and only dreamers get to experience that feeling.*

Provide Added Value

Then God said, "Let the waters swarm with fish and other life." *GENESIS 1:20*

Well beyond the halfway point of creation, at the start of day five, the Master Designer went back to the very beginning—to the water—to teach us another lesson about his personality.

God is a *maximizer*. He takes something that already exists and adds a new twist.

This is not senseless window dressing—God makes things better. By adding swarms of fish and other life to the oceans, he changed the waters from being formless and empty into an incredible ecosystem capable of sustaining life in his new creation.

The water had been around since the beginning of creation (see Genesis 1:2). But on the fifth day, God went back to maximize the waters by adding a valuable new dimension.

❖ *Is there a "body of water" in your organization that could be maximized by a fresh approach or an infusion of life? The critical element is to make sure the new twist actually provides an added value and makes the original idea more beneficial for users.*

Imagine the Future

Now go and call together all the elders of Israel. Tell them . . . I will lead you to a land flowing with milk and honey.   *EXODUS 3:16-17*

I was handling communications on the fund-raising committee for a church building program. Success was going to require sacrificial giving by the congregation.

During a discussion about how to communicate our plans, one committee member became frustrated at what he referred to as my "trying to put some kind of advertising spin on this thing."

"The people of God should give to his work because it's the right thing to do," he said.

I told him I wished it were that easy. The people may *know* what's right, but they will always do what they *feel,* and the only way to get them to *feel* is to burn an image of the future into their hearts.

The leaders of Israel knew they should follow God, but God knew they wouldn't do it unless they had a burning desire to live in a place "flowing with milk and honey."

❖ *Do people want to follow your lead?*

Use Fast Horses

The decree was written in the name of King Xerxes. . . . Mordecai sent the dispatches by swift messengers, who rode fast horses especially bred for the king's service.   *ESTHER 8:10*

The church board had prayerfully decided on a substantial goal for the fund-raising campaign. This incredible sum of money would require commitments from everyone in the congregation.

They erected a huge tent on Sunday morning and served breakfast to everyone. The pastor gave a compelling talk and told the people they would get a pledge card in Monday's mail. The board hoped folks would fill out the pledge card while their interest was still high from the Sunday celebration.

Someone decided to save money by mailing the pledge cards bulk rate instead of first class, so they arrived on Friday instead of Monday. Folks had been working all week. The flame of Sunday's meeting was extinguished, and the campaign fell short.

The king's message was important enough to warrant top-priority attention.

❖ *When your work is "mission critical," don't skimp on resources. When fast horses are required, use them.*

Are You Satisfied?

No matter how much we see, we are never satisfied. No matter how much we hear, we are not content. *ECCLESIASTES 1:8*

There's a delicate balance between satisfaction and complacency.

An effective leader must keep his or her eyes and ears open for new ideas. You must always be looking for opportunities beyond the horizon. Improving your organization's products or services is a top priority.

But some leaders run their organizations into the ground because they're never satisfied. Staff members lose passion for a project when they realize that no matter how good it is, the boss will not like it.

When nothing you do is good enough, you quit caring.

Perhaps the lesson is simply that leaders should assess their style and determine how it affects the mission.

Does your approach bring you closer to the mission? If not, some adjustment may be in order.

❖ *Are you satisfied with your own attitude about satisfaction?*

Lighten the Burden

Lighten the burden of those who work for you.   *ISAIAH 58:6*

This is a very complex issue, but far too many organizations are increasing their profit margins at the expense of their workers.

Two salaried employees are expected to do the work of three. Hourly workers are required to do more with less. Firms report record profits, but employees constantly fear that their positions will be eliminated to keep stockholders happy.

The organizations' leaders face tremendous pressure to bring the numbers in-line with bank ratios, investor requirements, and board directives, but God is crystal clear in his instructions.

His directive in Isaiah says nothing about profit margins, stockholder equity, or market pressure.

There is no justification for building your own nest on the back of another.

This isn't something you can fix quickly or on your own. Make a personal commitment to discuss this with your executive team within the next month.

❖ *Honestly weigh your corporate reality against God's simple instructions.*

Throw Out Your Net

Then he said, "Throw out your net on the right-hand side of the boat, and you'll get some!" So they did, and they couldn't haul in the net because there were so many fish in it.   *JOHN 21:6*

What could the son of a carpenter know about fishing that a boat full of seasoned fishermen did not?

There are two lessons here: First, Jesus is God, and he knew where the fish were. Second, the observations of those who are not in the thick of your situation are very valuable.

We aren't divine, so the practical lesson Jesus leaves us is the power of different perspectives.

These guys were drenched, exhausted, and discouraged. They had been doing what they thought was the right thing all night and had nothing to show for it. Jesus made a suggestion based on his view from the shore and, well, you know what happened.

How long has it been since you brought in someone with a unique perspective?

❖ *Maybe it's time to put your net down on the other side of the boat.*

Stop Being So Nice

You think you are so wise, but you enjoy putting up with fools! You put up with it when someone enslaves you, takes everything you have, takes advantage of you, takes control of everything, and slaps you in the face.   *2 CORINTHIANS 11:19-20*

When did "turn the other cheek" become a mandate to roll over and play dead rather than face up to bullies and chronic complainers?

Being a leader includes good stewardship of the time you have. That means doing something about people whose primary objective is to waste your time.

Paul urges us to avoid these people; he also scolds us for enjoying the distractions they bring.

You know who these people are. Confront them privately. Bring someone along and tell them they are no longer allowed to waste the time God has given you to accomplish his work.

Answer their questions and hear their concerns in private. Once their questions are answered, warn them that they will not be allowed to derail the next meeting with the same questions.

❖ *Stop being so nice.*

Know Your Team's Desires

When I raise my powerful hand and bring out the
Israelites, the Egyptians will know that I am the
LORD. *EXODUS 7:5*

Since the day of their birth, every Israelite in Egypt
had heard stories of "a land flowing with milk and
honey." Their souls must have ached with a desire to
go home.

They despised Pharaoh's oppression. After 430
years in Egypt, the promise that Pharaoh would fall
under God's hand resonated with them like a church
bell.

Your team's heartfelt desires are certainly less gran-
diose than crushing a tyrant, but they are no less
important. The most effective use of your time as a
leader will be the time you invest in getting to know
your staff.

What is going on in their lives? Were their education plans put on hold? Do their children need special care that a more flexible schedule might provide?
Has the accounting clerk always wanted to try his
hand at graphic design?

❖ *God knew the desires of his people's hearts.
Do you?*

Ask for Confirmation

Then Gideon said to God, "If you are truly going to use me to rescue Israel as you promised, prove it to me in this way." *JUDGES 6:36-37*

Gideon's famous request that God make the fleece wet and the ground dry was not motivated by defiance or disbelief. Gideon was eager to do God's will, and he wanted to make sure he was hearing God correctly.

Taking the time to ask a few questions gave Gideon the confidence he needed to move ahead.

I'm convinced that God included this story in his book to help us see the need to examine our own motives before moving ahead with controversial decisions:

> What is the business (or ministry) reason for doing this?
> If we don't do this, what happens?
> Are there other possible solutions?

Gideon wasn't looking for a way out. He wanted reassurance that he was making the right choice.

❖ *Look for evidence that your idea is a good one.*

Maintain Your Focus

Now I will tell you new things, secrets you have not yet heard. They are brand new, not things from the past. So you cannot say, "We knew that all the time!" *ISAIAH 48:6-7*

I describe people as being "heavily invested in the past" when they do everything they can to maintain the status quo—even if it means being uncomfortable.

Look out for these people when you present new ideas or investigate a problem.

"We knew that. Are you going to tell us anything new?"
"If you're aware of this, why haven't you corrected it?"
"We don't think it's a big problem."

God defines these folks as iron-necked, stubborn, and obstinate.

Bad news—they will always be around.
Good news—they are powerless against the inevitable. The future is going to happen despite them. They will eventually change or die trying not to.

❖ *Your job as a leader is to maintain your focus on the future so that when it does arrive, you are ready to step in and lead those who are willing to follow.*

UNIQUENESS

Stretch a Little

They are like trees planted along a riverbank, with roots that reach deep into the water. *JEREMIAH 17:8*

Besides the one in your hand, have you read any good books lately? What's the last good movie you saw? How long has it been since you had a nonbusiness lunch with a friend or had people over for a casual dinner at home?

There really is life outside work. It's the extra things we do—the nonwork stuff—that gives us roots and builds our foundations.

While building his case against Israel, God described a handful of people whose lives pleased him. "Their leaves stay green, and they never stop producing fruit" (Jeremiah 17:8).

God cares deeply about your profession.

He gifted you with unique skills and gave you a job because he knows how happy you are when you're productive.

However, obsessive attention to one thing—a job, school, church, or even a spouse—can produce very shallow roots that yield far less than the abundant life God wants for you.

❖ *Strike out. Try something new. Stretch your roots. Have fun.*

Orient New Employees

This is a record of the ancestors of Jesus the Messiah, a descendant of David and of Abraham.
MATTHEW 1:1

Janet took a job at a good company. After checking in with the human resources department, she was directed to the president's office for what she thought would be a brief greeting.

"Welcome to ABC Widgets, Janet. I'm Bob Widget. We're glad you're here. Before you start work, we want you to know all about us. It's my job to give you a tour of our company museum."

Bob led Janet to a room filled with memorabilia from the company's impressive past. Janet learned that the firm had been far more successful than her research had shown.

A list of former employees was a Who's Who of excellence in her field. She had big shoes to fill.

Like all Jewish kids of his day, Jesus knew where he had come from. He had a sense of who he was because he knew who had gone before him.

❖ *Do you give your new hires a sufficient background on their first day?*

Invest in What Works

Listen! A farmer went out to plant some seeds. As he scattered them across his field, some seeds fell on a footpath. . . . Other seeds fell on shallow soil. . . . Other seeds fell among thorns. . . . Still other seeds fell on fertile soil. *MATTHEW 13:3-8*

The candidate ran unopposed on the ballot. Nevertheless, she made public appearances and ran as if there were stiff opposition. In the end, she received 76 percent of the vote. Whom did the other 24 percent choose?

A few years ago, many people were reading the Left Behind fiction series. Each release became an overnight best seller. Despite tremendous success, overall sales were in the sixty-million range. This was less than half of the 125 million who consider themselves Christians in the United States.

My point is that you will never reach 100 percent of the people. However hard you try and however good your product is, some of your seeds will fall on infertile soil.

Jesus counseled his disciples to pay attention to the seeds that had a chance.

❖ *That's good advice for you, as well.*

Soar with the Eagles

Those who trust in the LORD will find new strength. They will soar high on wings like eagles.
ISAIAH 40:31

While hiking in the Big Horn Mountains, I was privileged to watch a bald eagle swoop down to snatch a rabbit.

The bird was awesome. While the rabbit struggled, the eagle pumped its massive wings and lifted off. I watched it until I could no longer see what was happening.

That's the image I've always had when reading this verse. I would get weary, trust God for strength, and he'd swoop down to carry me.

But read it again.

He gives me strength. It's *my* wings he makes strong. He's not giving me a ride. He's making me strong so I can finish the assignment.

This is great news for you. If you're like most leaders, you are a doer. The idea of being carried isn't high on your list of enjoyable activities. You like being in the driver's seat.

❖ *God knows how you're wired. He wants to renew your strength. He wants to watch you "soar high on wings like eagles."*

Reconsider Your Position

It is good for people to eat, drink, and enjoy their work under the sun during the short life God has given them, and to accept their lot in life.
ECCLESIASTES 5:18

I have a real problem with following a leader who seems uncomfortable in his or her role.

Allowing for different styles and levels of experience is one thing, but some folks in leadership positions just shouldn't be there, and they and the people around them all know it. Someone needs to do something about it, because this situation affects everyone.

God loves you and has a wonderful plan for your life. Are you sure his plan for you includes the leadership role you're in? Are you enjoying your work "during the short life God has given" you?

Have you accepted the plan he has for you, or have you been forced into a place you know you shouldn't be?

❖ *Stepping away from a leadership role is one of the toughest things you'll ever do, but it could be what God has in mind. Talk to him about it.*

Break Policy When Necessary

Zelophehad . . . had no sons . . . only daughters.
. . . These women came to . . . the Israelite leaders and said, "The LORD commanded Moses to give us a grant of land along with the men of our tribe." *JOSHUA 17:3-4*

One of Joshua's first tasks in the Promised Land was to portion out property. To prevent confusion, land was given to the males in each family.

This males-only policy worked until they came to a family in which the patriarch had no sons. His daughters had apparently not married into other families, so strict adherence to the policy would leave them with nothing.

Policies exist to standardize procedures; they are not core values, but guidelines along the way.

A chief duty of a leader is to decide when policies should be broken. Joshua gave the women their rightful inheritance. The goal was to fairly portion out the property, so policy was broken for the good of the mission.

❖ *Is a policy standing in your way?*

Inform Your Hunches

So all the men in the town council agreed . . . and every male in the town was circumcised. But three days later, when their wounds were still sore, two of Jacob's sons . . . took their swords and . . . slaughtered every male.   *GENESIS 34:24-26*

Talk about letting your passion get the best of you!

Passion is a good thing, and we need more passionate leaders, but every urge must be balanced with a dispassionate dose of due diligence.

Making key decisions based on passion without scrutiny is like running a marathon on nothing but Snickers and Kool-Aid. Empty calories will only sustain you for so long before you crash.

When passion appears to be running ahead of scrutiny, ask,

What's the business reason for doing this?

The answer may be, "My experience tells me this hunch is going to pay off, so I'd like to proceed."

❖ *Or it could be, "You're right. Let's do a bit more research to see if my hunch is correct."*

Finish What You Start

Then David ran over and pulled Goliath's sword from its sheath. David used it to kill [the giant] and cut off his head.   *1 SAMUEL 17:51*

Wow—I always thought David killed Goliath with a stone and a slingshot.

It is very difficult for some leaders to follow a project all the way to the end. The more visionary and future focused a person becomes, the harder it is for them to stay with a task until it's completed.

Be aware of how you introduce new ideas to your team.

You may thrive on vision, but many of the people you lead do not. They find satisfaction in getting a job done, and they don't appreciate being pulled off a task before it's finished. They're okay with looking at a new idea, but they want to know when they'll be able to complete the one they have already started.

How good are you at allowing people to finish what they have started?

❖ *Knocking the giant down is only the first step.*

Do the Right Thing

Ruth replied, "Don't ask me to leave you and turn back. Wherever you go, I will go; wherever you live, I will live." *RUTH 1:16*

The airport departure lounge was packed with vacation travelers, and it was well past the scheduled departure time. The Jetway had been damaged, and it would be hours before a repair crew could come to fix it.

That's when an airline suit showed up and whispered to the gate agent, who smiled as she announced,

"Well folks, as you know, our Jetway is broken, so we will take you down a flight of stairs and load the plane through the rear door. It's a bit unorthodox, but we want to get you on your way."

There's a difference between doing things right and doing the right thing.

Tradition required Ruth to go home and find a husband, but she did the right thing by staying with her dead husband's mother.

❖ *Don't let tradition interfere with doing the right thing.*

Honor Your Core Values

Samuel said, "What is this you have done?"
Saul replied, "I saw my men scattering from me, and you didn't arrive when you said you would. . . . So I felt compelled to offer the burnt offering myself before you came." *1 SAMUEL 13:11-12*

In Israel's hierarchy of core values, this one was near the top:

Only a priest could offer burnt sacrifices to the Lord.

Saul became impatient when things didn't go as planned. Samuel was delayed and things were heating up, so Saul followed the most expedient course. This incident cost Saul his throne.

Playing fast and loose with your organization's core values is a surefire way to set a course for failure. If quality is a core value, never compromise it to offer a lower price. If innovation is a priority, you'll reduce margins to offer the coolest ideas at an attractive price.

❖ *Make sure everyone on your team knows and understands your hierarchy of core values. Teach people to make decisions based on priorities rather than on the needs of the moment.*

Earn Your Team's Trust

We will do whatever you command us, and we will go wherever you send us.   *JOSHUA 1:16*

My friend Wayne Hastings once consulted on a project for DreamWorks, the Hollywood film-production company founded by three legendary entertainment moguls—Steven Spielberg, Jeffrey Katzenberg, and David Geffen.

The project was huge, and everyone was under extreme pressure. They were all working to the limits of their abilities.

In the midst of all this, Wayne noticed an even higher level of excitement one day and asked what the buzz was about. The response was, "Steven, Jeffrey, and David are in the boardroom developing some new ideas, and we can't wait to hear what they're planning for us."

These folks were running at full speed, but they were giddy with anticipation of new ideas because they respected their leaders.

Joshua had the same respect. The people saw his obvious commitment to their well-being and to the vision they had carried since Abraham's time. They would follow him anywhere.

❖ *Have you given your team a reason to trust in your ability to lead them?*

Take Your Time

For in six days, the LORD made the heavens, the earth, the sea, and everything in them.
EXODUS 20:11

God is the ultimate entrepreneur who creates opportunity out of nothing. He conceives new ideas and brings them to market. He blazes new trails where no one else has gone.

One thing God understands that many entrepreneurs don't is that things take time. We wake up in the morning with a new idea, and we're frustrated because it's still on the drawing board that afternoon.

"Why do we need to talk about this? Can't we just get it done?"

God could have shortened creation to the blink of an eye, but he played it out over several days to show us that there is value in the process. Coming up with a new idea is only the first of many steps in getting something done.

❖ *If your idea is really as good as you think it is, follow God's example and enjoy your creation as it unfolds, grows, and becomes a reality.*

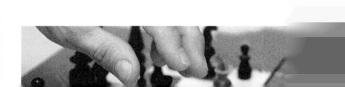

Tell People What You Do

No one lights a lamp and then puts it under a basket. Instead, a lamp is placed on a stand, where it gives light to everyone in the house.   *MATTHEW 5:15*

Take a moment to consider the benefit people receive when they use your organization's service or product.

Do you help them . . .

run faster?

live healthier?

save money?

complete a task?

navigate rough water?

If you provide real value to people, you are obligated to tell them about it. God gave you a unique gift, and he expects you to share it with others.

Hiding your lamp under a basket restricts the benefits to people who happen to cross your path by accident.

Jesus knew the value of his message; he encouraged his leadership team to take a proactive role in telling others about it.

If what you are doing can give light to people in darkness, step forward and let them know.

❖ *Don't shy away from publicity that will share your good ideas with those who can benefit from them.*

Use Street Teams

John said to Jesus, "Teacher, we saw someone using your name to cast out demons, but we told him to stop because he wasn't in our group."

"Don't stop him!" Jesus said, "No one who performs a miracle in my name will soon be able to speak evil of me." *MARK 9:38-39*

A marketing strategy known as "street teams" uses loosely organized groups of people to unofficially represent an organization within their social networks.

Street teams are effective because the representative (or captain) is motivated by a strong affinity with the product rather than by monetary reward.

Street-team captains are intensely loyal to their products. Marketers use words such as *advocate* and *evangelist* to describe them.

Jesus knew the value of people who were tuned in to his mission but operated outside of his "official" team. He encouraged them to strike out on their own to spread the news.

❖ *You probably have a group of customers or fans who would be effective evangelists for your mission. Encourage them to perform a miracle in your name.*

Keep On Doing the Right Thing

Let's not get tired of doing what is good.
GALATIANS 6:9

The village of Lombard, Illinois, owns a historic theater and shopping area worth millions of dollars because one organization did "what is good." The story was reported by *Charisma News Service*:

> Big Idea Productions is giving a 2.5-acre site to the community after backing out of plans to develop it. President Bob Patin says, "It was purely an effort to live out in our behavior the values that we espouse in our work. . . . Do the right thing, no matter what.
>
> "Our [changing plans] derailed downtown development and hurt the town's pride," said Patin. "Typically in business, if you make a mistake you cut your losses and move forward. Here, we looked at who we are and what we stand for and said the proof had to come out of our own wallet."

Paul cautions against selfishness that flourishes in a traditional environment of rigid adherence to policy.

❖ *You can do things the right way, or you can do the right thing. The choice you make depends on how you define and measure success.*

Practice Mutuality with Your Staff

When people work, their wages are not a gift, but something they have earned.   *ROMANS 4:4*

At my first real job, the owner delivered paychecks by holding them tightly in his hand until the employee said, "Thank you."

When I got up the nerve to ask why he did this, his answer was, "I want to know that you're grateful for the opportunity to work here."

He believed he was doing us all a favor by allowing us to work for him, but I don't think he ever considered the flip side.

We made it possible for him to operate a business.

Paul distinguishes between the relationship you have with God and the one you have with your staff.

God's provision is a gift, based on faith, for which we should be grateful.

Wages are part of a mutually beneficial contract between a worker and an employer. Both should have an equal stake and reward in the relationship.

❖ *Do you approach the issue of wages with an attitude of mutual respect and value?*

Issue New Policy with Care

"Let a curse fall on anyone who eats before evening—before I have full revenge on my enemies." So no one ate anything all day, even though they had all found honeycomb. *1 SAMUEL 14:24-25*

Saul wanted his army to remain focused on a critical battle. Stopping to prepare food would distract them, so he issued a ridiculous policy about not eating anything, even though there was food readily available.

A more effective order would have been, "Our objective is to keep fighting until we are victorious. Don't let anything slow you down."

You have probably issued similar orders:

✦ "We spend too much on overnight delivery. From now on, *nothing* goes overnight."

✦ "We're giving away too much margin. *Every* sale must have a minimum margin of X percent."

✦ "I called in and the phone rang and rang before someone answered. *Every* incoming phone call *must* be answered before the third ring."

Obeying snap edicts to the letter can hamper your team's ability to efficiently meet your goals.

❖ *Don't turn good intentions into big trouble—issue new policy with care.*

Listen to Your People

The people broke in and said to Saul, "Jonathan has won this great victory for Israel. Should he die? . . ." So the people rescued Jonathan, and he was not put to death. *1 SAMUEL 14:45*

On occasion, you need to listen to the people you're leading. They, in turn, need to speak up when you've made a poor decision.

It's a two-way street.

People need to speak, and leaders need to listen. The mission suffers if either side fails in their responsibilities.

Saul had issued a ridiculous decree that would mandate the death of his son. He knew he had made a mistake, but he refused to reverse his ruling.

The people spoke up. They saw the situation from a different perspective and presented a strong case in Jonathan's defense. Saul backed down, and Jonathan was spared.

The people spoke, the leader listened, and a tragic mistake was avoided.

❖ *Do you encourage your staff to challenge your decisions? Do you listen when they see things from a different perspective?*

Observe the Golden Rule

Do to others whatever you would like them to do to you.   *MATTHEW 7:12*

We call it the Golden Rule.

The concept of treating others as we wish to be treated is found in nearly every religion, from Native American spirituality to Zoroastrianism. Seneca, Plato, and Socrates taught their versions of it. Even those without any religious affiliation ascribe to "the ethics of reciprocity."

It is simple, elegant, straightforward—and easily ignored or taken for granted.

The simplicity of the Golden Rule can lull us into a false sense that we are doing okay. Our minds automatically agree with the words, but are we living up to the standard Jesus described on the Mount of Olives?

Will you accept a twenty-four-hour challenge?

Between now and this time tomorrow, concentrate on the essence of this idea. Look for ways in which you may be treating someone in a manner that's inconsistent with your desire to live by the Golden Rule.

❖ *Think deeply about your leadership style. Do you really treat everyone as you would like to be treated?*

Resist Shortsighted "Solutions"

For everything that is hidden will eventually be brought into the open, and every secret will be brought to light. *MARK 4:22*

How many corporate scandals would be avoided if leaders paid attention to this simple fact? How many marriages would be saved? How much embarrassment avoided?

The temptation to lie, cheat, or steal is driven by the rush of gratification such actions purport to provide.

Breaking the rules opens the door to a quick reward, but there is always a price to be paid.

Jesus couldn't have put it any clearer—your actions, motives, and decisions will be revealed. Someone will pay the price, sometime, somewhere.

Perhaps you're tempted to take a shortcut. Here's a suggestion: Take a moment to imagine the headlines that will be written when your actions come to light. While you're thinking about the immediate pleasure you'll receive, think also about the pain you'll feel when everything is brought into the open.

❖ *The power of pleasure is very strong. Is the short-term gain worth the long-term pain?*

Make Strategic Plans

I will make Pharaoh's heart stubborn so I can multiply my miraculous signs and wonders in the land of Egypt. *EXODUS 7:3*

God is a master strategist.

Each of the seven plagues enacted a slightly different indignity on Pharaoh. Each built on the preceding calamity, and each was perfectly timed to achieve the maximum effect.

It was a step-by-step plan. The chapters of Exodus following today's text outline the plagues as they unfold around Pharaoh.

There is real pleasure in developing a detailed strategic plan and watching it blossom. God could have simply rubbed Pharaoh into the sand, but we're told that God wanted to teach Pharaoh a lesson about his sovereignty.

I think he also wanted to set an example for us. Do you take the time to draw up strategic plans? Do you have a step-by-step outline of your next major campaign?

❖ *God did. You should too.*

Identify Your Champions

Whenever the LORD raised up a judge over Israel, he was with that judge and rescued the people from their enemies. . . . But when the judge died, the people returned to their corrupt ways.
JUDGES 2:18-19

My company had negotiated a substantial contract with a major corporation, and work was just beginning when the vice president who had approved the deal for our client resigned and left the company.

The client paid a cancellation fee and stopped the project because the person who left had been the champion, and without him, no one felt compelled to continue.

Champions are people to whom the entire organization can look for vision and motivation on a particular task. They're the cheerleaders. They ignite the light at the end of the tunnel.

When God raised up a judge, the people saw that person as a champion.

Champions are not always members of the executive or leadership team. Allowing a nonmanagement staff person to champion a project can be a great way to groom them for more responsibility in the future.

❖ *Champions should be visible. Who are the champions for your key projects?*

Mind Your Own Business

Why worry about a speck in your friend's eye when you have a log in your own? *LUKE 6:41*

One of the most fruitless distractions for an organization is paying too much attention to their competition. It's certainly important to know what they're doing, but some leaders take this to the extreme. They spend more time analyzing the other guy's decisions than they do making their own.

The result is a crop of reactive and shortsighted ideas.

Jesus reminds us that our perspectives are often out of alignment to the point where we see tiny specks of dust as much larger than they really are. We focus so intently on the speck of dust that we completely lose sight of our own, much larger, internal issues.

Throughout the Gospels, Jesus emphasizes the wisdom of maintaining a focus on our own agendas. He teaches us to focus on problems that we are responsible for and not to waste time on those we can't control.

❖ *As Grandma used to say, "Pay attention to your own knitting."*

Cater to Diversity

I am writing to all of you in Rome who are loved by God and are called to be his own holy people. *ROMANS 1:7*

We get about one hundred cable TV channels at my house.

On the History Channel, commercials feature products for older people—electric chairs, supplemental insurance, and hearing aids.

Over at MTV, the pitch is for athletic shoes, energy drinks, and iPods.

Targeted marketing isn't new—the apostle Paul's approach to people was often based on demographics.

Paul presented the same gospel of Christ in each of his letters, including this one to the Christians in Rome, but he wrote each epistle in a style suited to his intended audience.

Each audience your organization serves has its own language. Your message is more effective when it's tailored to resonate with each intended recipient.

Make a list of the groups you want to reach.

What is unique about each one?

What does each group like about your product?

Do you sell more of one item to a certain group? Why?

❖ *Pay attention to the diversity of your audience.*

Stick to the Truth

These people are stubborn rebels who refuse to pay attention to the LORD's instructions. . . . They tell the prophets, "Don't tell us what is right. Tell us nice things. Tell us lies. Forget all this gloom."
ISAIAH 30:9-11

A well-established company was losing its market share in some key categories. My assignment was to measure customer satisfaction.

My research pointed to problems requiring immediate action. I also found some highlights on which to build a revival. The news wasn't good, but it was truthful.

At my formal presentation, a senior executive stood up, shouted a mild expletive, and accused me of manufacturing the results to ensure a continuing assignment. I hadn't done this.

Although I am rarely cursed, his reaction was common. Those who significantly invest in the status quo often malign the messengers of truth. I showed him the facts, but he refused to accept the reality that his company needed to change. Six months later he resigned.

Isaiah faced a similar reaction when he spoke the truth to the Israelites.

❖ *How do you respond when the truth hurts?*

Don't Cheat Your Employees

I will put you on trial. I am eager to witness against all sorcerers and adulterers and liars. I will speak against those who cheat employees of their wages. *MALACHI 3:5*

In one breath, God voices his displeasure with people who practice witchcraft, break their marriage vows, tell lies, and cheat employees.

What constitutes cheating a worker out of his or her wages?

Are workers being cheated when

+ executives receive comfortable bonus checks the same week layoff notices go out to rank-and-file wage earners?
+ you delay a deserved salary increase until they ask for it?
+ top managers are paid hundreds of times more than the average workers' hourly rate?
+ married men are paid more than single women for the same job because the guy has a family to support?

Cheating can be defined as taking unfair advantage of someone. God says he will witness against those who do so.

❖ *Examine your own employee-wage practices. How do they stand up under the scrutiny of God's judgment?*

Reflect on Your Own Actions

Do not judge others, and you will not be judged. Do not condemn others.   LUKE 6:37

Howard is a friend and mentor who occasionally offers me a dose of painful but necessary advice.

We met when he was brought in to consult my department. I wanted to put my best foot forward, so I spent most of our first session telling him all the things I was not:

"I'm not like so-and-so who doesn't care about people's feelings."

"Or like so-and-so who makes rash decisions based on personal preference."

"And certainly not like so-and-so who overspends her budget."

Finally, Howard stopped me and said, "You've told me all the things you're not. Now, tell me something you are. Don't tell me what you don't do; tell me what you do."

Jesus would prefer that we deal with our own issues. He knows how easily we point a finger at others without seeing similar faults of our own, so he tells us not to judge others.

❖ *Measure yourself against a standard of personal accountability, and reflect on your own actions.*

Rely on the Holy Spirit

I want to do what is right, but I can't. I want to do what is good, but I don't. I don't want to do what is wrong, but I do it anyway.   *ROMANS 7:18-19*

Are you a master of procrastination? Is it impossible for you to relax? Maybe you're a raging perfectionist, or a person who makes too many mistakes.

Pushy or timid? Ego driven or lacking in confidence?

We all do things we'd rather not do. God tells us, through Paul, that he understands.

Paul had a firm perception of his real strengths and weaknesses. He knew where he was deficient and took steps to mitigate his limitations. He didn't let his concern take control of his attitude. Instead, he relied on the Holy Spirit to guide his actions. He never gave up trying to do what was good.

❖ *God cares deeply about your professional behavior. He wants to help you win the battle over laziness, indecision, egoism, and impatience. He understands your frustration, and he's ready to step in—whenever you're ready to make the call.*

Anticipate Trouble

Abram said to his wife, Sarai, "Look, you are a very beautiful woman. When the Egyptians see you, they will say, 'This is his wife. Let's kill him; then we can have her!' So please tell them you are my sister." *GENESIS 12:11-13*

One of the things I appreciate about the Bible is that it doesn't gloss over the dumb things its heroes do—and this is certainly one of them. Nevertheless, Abram's actions provide a valuable lesson:

Anticipate trouble.

As a leader, it's your responsibility to look beyond the horizon to see what's coming up. Let your managers handle the day-to-day activities while you practice the future.

With key members of your executive team, talk about what you will do if

- a major supplier suddenly goes out of business.
- new government regulations change the way you distribute your product.
- society changes and people no longer want or need your type of service.

❖ *By practicing what you would do in each of these—and countless other—cases, you'll be better prepared to act confidently if one of them becomes a reality.*

Maximize Your Team's Skills

Then Miriam the prophet, Aaron's sister . . .
EXODUS 15:20

If there were a contest for Worst Home Handyman, I would be a strong contender. Geoff, on the other hand, always knows how to do things right. When he comes to paint, there are twenty different brushes and tools in his box, and he chooses the one that is precisely suited to the job at hand.

He doesn't place more value on one tool than another. He doesn't ignore a particular tool when it is clearly the right one for a specific project. A key element in Geoff's success is his ability to use each tool to its maximum potential.

Miriam was a woman. In the strictly patriarchal Jewish society, God chose a woman to lead the people because she was obviously best suited for the job.

One of your responsibilities as a leader is to maximize the skills of every team member, regardless of their age, gender, shape, size, or color. It's easy to rationalize not doing this, so take a moment to seriously consider your practice in this area.

❖ *You've been blessed by God with a toolbox of people with diverse skills. Are you allowing each of them to contribute to their fullest potential?*

Find the Sweet Spot

Jesus sent out the twelve apostles with these instructions: "Don't go to the Gentiles . . . but only to the people of Israel." *MATTHEW 10:5-6*

A baseball bat has an area called the sweet spot. The September 1998 edition of the *American Journal of Physics* locates it "about 17 cm from the end of the barrel, where the shock of the impact . . . is reduced to such an extent that the batter is almost unaware of the collision."

Players who hit the ball in the sweet spot are reportedly able to drive it farther. This isn't the only place on the bat to hit the ball, but doing so increases the chance of success.

New products or ideas may have broad appeal, but you'll increase their potential for success if you identify those most likely to buy what you have to sell.

Jesus' message was for everyone, but he began in the sweet spot, with those who already had an affinity with his Father, Yahweh.

❖ *Don't spread your initial marketing efforts over too wide an audience. Look for the sweet spot and swing for the fence.*

Fine-Tune Your Product Descriptions

If I could speak all the languages of earth and of angels, but didn't love others, I would only be a noisy gong or a clanging cymbal.
1 CORINTHIANS 13:1

If God were an organization, this chapter might be the page in the employee manual that explains what makes the product unique:

> At Yahweh, Inc., our number one product is love. Everything we do has love as its first ingredient. As a Yahweh staff member, you should be able to answer the question, "So what is this thing called love?"

Paul's love chapter gives a simple, complete, and powerful answer.

Do you have a similar way of describing your primary product or service? Most organizations need work in this area. Their product descriptions are too detailed or too vague.

❖ *Find someone who isn't familiar with your product and ask them to read your material. Then ask them to describe what you do in their own words. If they get it wrong, you have a problem.*

Admit Your Mistakes

I restore the crushed spirit of the humble and revive the courage of those with repentant hearts.
ISAIAH 57:15

Quick—stop for a second and name the last time a public figure stepped up to the podium and admitted doing something wrong or making a mistake.

The clock is ticking—buzzzz—time's up.

I'll bet you couldn't think of one. If you did, you probably can't think of another.

Now start a list of people who owe the world an apology. Set a time limit, or you'll be at it all day.

"I'm sorry. I made a mistake."

It goes against our nature to admit that we've messed up, but God promises to restore and revive those who do.

It makes good sense. Failing to admit a mistake stalls the recovery process. If it has gone too far, people already have a hunch you're the culprit. They're just waiting for you to fess up so they can move on.

Do you need restoration? Are you ready for revival?

❖ *Start the ball rolling right now.*

Nourish Your Mind

The people of Israel feed on the wind. HOSEA 12:1

In the 2004 film documentary *Super Size Me,* Morgan Spurlock eats nothing but fast food for thirty days, with a profoundly negative effect on his physical health.

Just as your physical health is affected by the food you eat, what you feed your mind affects your intellectual health.

Our minds are often centered on the consumption of garbage.

God complained to Hosea that his people were not feeding their minds at all. They weren't taking in garbage—they weren't taking in anything.

Unfortunately, this malnutrition of the mind is common. In our rush to get things done, we relegate intellectual health to the back burner. We don't take time to feed our minds because our to-do lists are too long.

Where does intellectual nourishment stand on your list of priorities?

❖ *Your mind is a terrible thing to waste.*

Rattle the Box a Bit

Here are the names of the twelve apostles:
. . . Matthew (the tax collector) . . . Simon (the
zealot). . . .   *MATTHEW 10:2-4*

Does everyone on your team get along? Are the votes
always unanimous? Do you brag about how your
people hang out with each other on the weekends?

You need to rattle the box a bit.

Teams of people who play nicely in the same
sandbox are great at maintaining status quo, but they
aren't very good at generating new ideas.

Jesus was about to turn the world upside down.
For his team, he chose two men who were on opposite ends of the political and economic spectrums of
their day.

Simon was a Jewish nationalist who hated everything about Rome and zealously desired to destroy
it. Matthew was a Roman tax collector. These two
men had lived their entire lives hating everything
the other stood for. Can you imagine the dialogue
between them?

Jesus either made a colossal mistake, or he understood the value of different ideas.

❖ *How diverse is your team?*

Avoid Double Binds

No one can serve two masters. *LUKE 16:13*

The customer service team was frustrated. Their once legendary performance was suffering because they were getting double messages from senior management.

The executive team had decided that CS reps should report monthly on critical issues they had handled. The concept was great, but it resulted in disaster.

From the beginning, each monthly report was met with such a fierce level of defensiveness that the reps drew straws to determine who would be sacrificed in the boardroom.

Jesus understood that loyalties cannot be divided evenly. In this case, the customer service reps were being asked to serve two masters:

1. Do whatever it takes to serve the customer, and
2. Protect the company from unreasonable customer service requests.

The confusion caused the reps to despise the organization they had once been proud of. This downward spiral ended with every one of the reps leaving in less than a year.

❖ *Does your organization send double messages that confuse and frustrate people?*

Enjoy Your Work

I saw that there is nothing better for people than to be happy in their work.   *ECCLESIASTES 3:22*

The little company had grown faster than anyone imagined possible. One year, the annual picnic was held in the founder's backyard. The following year, they rented the city park and hired a caterer.

The founder stood on a picnic table and raised his hands to bless the meal.

"Before I pray for the food, let me thank you *all* for being here. This last year has been incredible, and I promise that I will do everything I can to ensure that we continue to have as much fun working together as we do right now."

The author of Ecclesiastes reminds us that no one will bring us back to enjoy life after we die, so we should be happy in our work.

Perhaps the best investment you can make in your organization is to follow the example of the company founder who vowed to help his team enjoy their time with him.

❖ *What do you do to make your place fun?*

Acknowledge Incremental Success

There he built another altar and . . . worshiped the LORD. *GENESIS 12:8*

Abram's mission was to explore the territory God had promised to his descendants. He set out from his native country, fixed his sights on his destination, and celebrated his progress at every stop along the way by erecting an altar to Yahweh.

A friend of mine was project manager for a unit at Apple computers just before the first Macintosh computers were brought to market. He describes the pace as furious. There was a high stress level because failure wasn't an option.

When they hit a major milestone late one night, a lot of work still remained to be done. But the manager handed out rubber-band guns and yelled, "Don't fire 'til you see the whites of their eyes" as he led his group in a ten-minute rubber-band war.

Their renewed energy level carried the team happily through the next task.

❖ *Mark incremental success with visible signs of celebration.*

Establish Common Ground

But Jesus said, "It should be done, for we must carry out all that God requires." So John agreed to baptize him.   *MATTHEW 3:15*

What a great example of Jesus' ability to honor the past while forging new ground!

When Jesus came to John the Baptist to be baptized, John refused him, saying, "I am the one who needs to be baptized by you" (Matthew 3:14).

It was the very beginning of Jesus' public ministry. He was aware that his privacy would soon be shattered and that people would begin to scrutinize his every move. He knew he'd be shaking up the marbles over the next few years, but at that moment, he started inside the box by following tradition and doing "all that God requires."

When you're planning to lead people into new territory, look for a comfortable entry point.

Find some common ground from which to step off.

❖ *Give people a reason to trust you by showing that you know what's important to them.*

Seek God's Kingdom

Jesus said, "That is why I tell you not to worry about everyday life—whether you have enough food to eat or enough clothes to wear. For life is more than food, and your body more than clothing. Look at the ravens. They don't plant or harvest or store food in barns, for God feeds them. And you are far more valuable to him than any birds! Can all your worries add a single moment to your life? And if worry can't accomplish a little thing like that, what's the use of worrying over bigger things? Look at the lilies. . . . They don't work or make their clothing, yet Solomon in all his glory was not dressed as beautifully as they are. And if God cares so wonderfully for flowers . . . , he will certainly care for you. Why do you have so little faith? And don't be concerned about what to eat and what to drink. Don't worry about such things. These things dominate the thoughts of unbelievers all over the world, but your Father already knows your needs. Seek the Kingdom of God above all else, and he will give you everything you need.   *LUKE 12:22-31*

❖ *Spend every spare minute today thinking and praying about these verses.*

Let Righteousness Cover You

All who heard me praised me. All who saw me spoke well of me. For I assisted the poor in their need and the orphans who required help. I helped those without hope, and they blessed me. . . . Everything I did was honest. Righteousness covered me like a robe, and I wore justice like a turban.   JOB 29:11-14

Over the years, easily a thousand résumés have come across my desk, but I've never seen one with the qualifications that Job provides here.

What an incredible statement about what's important in Job's life! I don't get the sense that he was boasting of an accomplishment or trying to make himself look good. He was describing the lifestyle he had before he lost all his possessions to a series of calamities beyond his control.

Find time to read all of Job 29.

❖ *What are your personal goals? Would you want someone like Job on your team? Are you able to make a similar statement on your résumé?*

Have Fun Together

When it was all over, the king gave a banquet for all the people, from the greatest to the least.
ESTHER 1:5

In an age of tight budgets and close attention to the bottom line, it is tempting to eliminate company picnics and other seemingly frivolous events, but these special days are worth far more than the expense of hosting them.

Xerxes was a hugely successful monarch, with a kingdom extending from India to Ethiopia. One element of his success must have been his regular practice of bringing people together for banquets and celebrations. The book of Esther reads like the celebrity column of a major newspaper.

These people knew how to have fun.

One of your roles as a leader is to maintain good levels of productivity. You want to be a good steward of the human resources you've been given.

People who enjoy each other's company tend to work well together.

❖ *Does someone on your team have the responsibility of finding ways for people to have fun together? Do you have a vice president of Fun and Games? You should.*

Use New Wineskins

No one puts new wine into old wineskins. For the old skins would burst from the pressure, spilling the wine and ruining the skins.   *MATTHEW 9:17*

Albert Einstein is generally credited with one of my favorite axioms:

Insanity is doing the same thing over and over and expecting different results.

Jesus' disciples were criticized for not observing many of the traditional religious practices of their day. People asked Jesus why his followers didn't do things the way they had always been done.

His response was simple:

If you want different results, you need to make changes.

Have you been trying to fix problems in your organization by using the same tools that got you where you are? Has your response to being stuck been to do the same things bigger, faster, or more often?

Old wineskins aren't bad. They have produced great wine. But it is time to make a new kind of wine and move in a different direction.

❖ *The old ideas are comfortable, familiar, and safe. They're also a surefire remedy for maintaining the status quo. Is that what you want?*

Paint Word Pictures

We will all be transformed! It will happen in a moment, in the blink of an eye, when the last trumpet is blown. For when the trumpet sounds, those who have died will be raised to live forever. And we who are living will also be transformed.

1 CORINTHIANS 15:51-52

A radio station where I worked featured a nightly program from the golden days of radio. We played dramas, comedies, and old news reports filled with mental images of police shoot-outs, stuff falling out of Fibber McGee's closet, and the Hindenburg bursting into flames.

The words left unforgettable images on the canvas of my mind.

Paul understood that getting folks to hear what you have to say is just the first step. He reached past their intellect and connected with their emotions by painting pictures on the hearts of his readers.

He didn't just tell them about the Rapture; he used words that helped them to see it, feel it, and long for its advent.

How well do you tell stories?

❖ *If a picture is worth a thousand words, then words that paint pictures are priceless.*

Celebrate Your Differences

In his grace, God has given us different gifts for doing certain things well.   *ROMANS 12:6*

Look closely at the three points Paul is making in this passage:

1. God has given us different gifts for doing certain things. Each person on your team has unique talents. All are better at some things than others—and that's okay.
2. We are expected to use our respective gifts to the best of our ability. God wants us to do things well.
3. The fact that you and I are different proves God's love for each one of us. He loves us enough to make each of us unique.

As a leader, it's often easier to shoot for uniformity. Things run more smoothly when everyone agrees and the votes are unanimous, but that's not what God intended. Our differences are not the result of an error; we are the way we are because God—in his grace—gave us diversity.

❖ *Get your team together and list your different opinions and approaches. Then honor God by celebrating your differences.*

Maintain Confidentiality

I slipped out during the night, taking only a few others with me. I had not told anyone about the plans God had put in my heart for Jerusalem.

NEHEMIAH 2:12

When my wife's family gets together to play cards, there's always someone who can't hold his cards without everyone else seeing what's in his hand. This person (okay, it's me) needs to hold his cards "close to the vest."

Nehemiah provides a good example of this leadership principal as he describes his inspection of Jerusalem's wall in the middle of the night.

He wasn't doing anything improper or unethical, but it was critical that his plans not be made public until he had finished his research. There was no benefit to be gained by sharing his strategy until it was locked into place and ready to go.

Every leader needs a small group of people in whom to confide. Ideas need to be tossed around and refined before they are made public. Announcing half-baked plans is a good recipe for failure.

❖ *Do you have a select group of confidants?*

Do Something Incredible

The man went and spread the word, proclaiming to everyone what had happened. As a result, large crowds soon surrounded Jesus. . . . People from everywhere kept coming to him.   MARK 1:45

Perhaps you've heard the term *Viral Marketing*. Wikipedia defines it as "marketing techniques that seek to exploit pre-existing social networks to produce exponential increases in brand awareness, through viral processes similar to the spread of an epidemic."

Viral marketing spreads quickly because it is passed along by people who have been touched by a product or service in unusual ways.

The leper that Jesus healed told his friends what had happened because he couldn't keep quiet. There wasn't any compensation—he wasn't a paid endorser, just a raving fan.

There are two ways to spread the message of your product or service. You can buy advertising (ads, public relations, promotions, etc.), or you can do something so incredible that people just can't help but tell their friends, who tell their friends, who tell their friends—until "people from everywhere" come to see you.

❖ Is your organization doing anything incredible?

Rehearse Your Speeches

The Lord was pleased with the aroma of the sacrifice and said to himself, "I will never again curse the ground because of the human race."
GENESIS 8:21

In their book *Now, Discover Your Strengths*, Marcus Buckingham and Donald O. Clifton describe the process Colin Powell goes through before making a major speech. The former general and secretary of state is a poster child for "cool, calm, and collected" in any situation. Part of his secret, according to Buckingham and Clifton, is the way he reviews his notes prior to stepping onto the platform.

Consider that in light of God's example at the conclusion of Noah's story.

The Lord was getting ready to make a major announcement, and he spoke to himself before he spoke to Noah. God clearly doesn't need to practice, so the example must be there for our benefit.

If the announcement you are preparing is important, then it's worthy of some practice.

Practice your speech.

If you'll be taking questions from the audience, have someone toss tough questions at you.

❖ *Be prepared.*

Use What Is Available

"But we have only five loaves of bread and two fish!" they answered.

"Bring them here," he said.   *MATTHEW 14:17-18*

My company produced a thirty-minute video as part of a national retail promotion.

Ten days before the launch, I received disturbing news: Three seconds of the tape were defective, so the audio had a slight hiccup. You could still understand the speaker, but it wasn't perfect.

The problem had already been fixed, and all tapes made after this were okay. What about the two-thousand tapes with the slight imperfection?

Waiting until we had enough good tapes would mean missing the start date and ruining the campaign, so I decided to ship the imperfect tapes with a note that they would be replaced as soon as new tapes were available.

The disciples were waiting until everything was just right. Jesus looked at a bigger picture—the people needed to eat, so he went with what was available.

❖ *Does your pursuit of perfection get in the way of the mission? Are you waiting for a complete meal when some fish and rolls would be enough?*

Be Strong and Take Action

Get up, for it is your duty to tell us how to proceed in setting things straight. We are behind you, so be strong and take action. *EZRA 10:4*

This one makes me chuckle—it's so typical.

Ezra had just led the Israelite remnant back to Jerusalem, and now he was exhorting them to confess their sins and purify their lives.

As the people begged Ezra to get up and do his duty, I wonder if they weren't actually saying, "Okay, Ezra, if you want us to do this, you need to step out in front because we are too scared, lazy, or indifferent to do it ourselves."

Some people need strong leaders because they don't want to make decisions and would rather have someone tell them what to do. They aren't particular about where the leader goes, and they are easily led astray by unscrupulous shepherds.

Pay special attention to these folks. Make sure they hear your voice.

❖ *Poeple are looking for someone they can stand behind, so "be strong and take action."*

Focus Your Attention

God is not a God of disorder but of peace.
1 CORINTHIANS 14:33

Does this mean that God wants me to clean my desk?

I watched a news report recently about a home that had been overtaken by a massive swarm of honeybees. Images on the TV showed millions of bees crawling over each other in what appeared to be utter chaos.

An expert explained that the bees really did have a purpose. For an unknown reason, the colony's queen bee had left her hive and was nesting in the attic of the home. All the other bees were there to support and provide for the queen.

What looked like disorder to the casual observer was actually quite intentional, by honeybee standards. Despite appearances to the contrary, they were internally focused on a critical purpose.

So, what about my desk?

I think God is less concerned about the outward appearance of disorder and more concerned about the focus of my attention. Throughout his book, God sets plans and follows them. He is proactive and strategic, not reactive.

❖ *Does your activity have a purpose?*

Notice God's Work

We know that God causes everything to work together for the good of those who love God and are called according to his purpose for them.

ROMANS 8:28

Examples of this passage in action run the gamut from hardly believable to barely noticeable. Some people practice what a friend calls "God watching," which is looking back over a situation to identify God's touch in it.

The more my friend looks for God in past events, the easier it is for him to see God's hand at work as things unfold. It's like wearing a special set of glasses that reveal God in the midst of all the dust and noise.

This promise can help you make confident decisions when the future is unclear. Knowing that God is superintending the process reduces the worry of making a bad choice or going in the wrong direction.

The apostle Paul says the Holy Spirit prays on our behalf when we don't know what to ask God for.

❖ *There's no reason to feel as if the decision is all on your shoulders.*

Make Good Alliances

Can two people walk together without agreeing on the direction?   *AMOS 3:3*

I have been honored to facilitate discussions between companies that are forming strategic alliances. These unions are most successful when both sides are completely transparent about their objectives for the partnership.

When both companies understand what the other is trying to accomplish, they can more easily use their unique competencies to achieve common solutions.

The prophet Amos is delivering a message from the Lord to the people of Israel. God is warning them of the consequences of not walking in step with his lead.

Strategic alliances make good business sense. Fast-food chains and Hollywood film producers do it on a grand scale.

Maybe it's your clothing store and a health club, or your furniture shop and a remodeling contractor, or your children's dental practice and a day-care center. The possibilities are endless.

❖ *Agreeing on where you want to go is a good place to start.*

Have a Unified Purpose

In early autumn, when the Israelites had settled in their towns, all the people assembled in Jerusalem with a unified purpose.   *EZRA 3:1*

The Israelites had just been through a terrible chapter in their history. After being exiled for a generation to a foreign land, a remnant were now returning home to rebuild their capital city.

Everyone pitched in on this community-wide effort. Adversity hadn't destroyed their spirits, but strengthened them.

The catalyst for this renewed resolve was a leader who refused to let the current situation destroy his vision for the future.

Perhaps your organization is facing tough times. Don't lose sight of your vision. Assess your situation and plan to fix the problem.

Always keep your eye on the prize.

Rebuilding the city wasn't easy. There were many obstacles along the way, but the people were encouraged by a leader who helped them see what would result from their hard work. They flourished under his leadership.

❖ *There's nothing like adversity to align a group of people on a mission.*

Follow Your Convictions

Blessed are those who don't feel guilty for doing something they have decided is right. But if you have doubts about whether or not you should eat something, you are sinning if you go ahead and do it. For you are not following your convictions.

ROMANS 14:22-23

It's tough being an effective leader these days, and even more difficult to be a Christian leader because of all the extra standards imposed by people who strongly resemble the Pharisees.

✦ Don't do business on Sunday.
✦ Don't serve wine at client-appreciation events.
✦ Open every meeting or conference call with prayer.
✦ Put Bible verses at the bottom of all your e-mails.
✦ Play only Christian music on your office radio.

There's nothing wrong with any of these, and there's nothing wrong with doing the opposite. Paul makes it clear that there is a wide range of acceptable options. What really matters is the personal account you will give to God for your decisions (see Romans 14:4).

❖ *As you lead, keep your eyes on the long-range prize and step over all the senseless stuff people throw at your feet.*

Correct Your Course

Go back to what you heard and believed at first;
hold to it firmly. *REVELATION 3:3*

Outdoorplaces.com has this to say about getting lost
in the wilderness:

> "One of our worst traits as humans is our abil-
> ity to deny to ourselves that we are lost. We
> wander around [until] the unfamiliar becomes
> familiar and we become disoriented."

Experts say that the key to avoiding making a bad
situation worse in the wilderness is to stop immediately and get down to the business of surviving.

Your leadership responsibilities include making
sure the organization stays on the path to your objective. Make immediate corrections if it begins to stray.

Jesus sent a wake-up call to the church at Sardis.
He urged their leaders to "strengthen what little
remains" (Revelation 3:2) before they ran out of time.

The longer you wait, the more drastic the fix will
need to be.

> "The moment you realize you're lost—take
> a deep breath and plan your next moves care-
> fully. What you do in the first hour will have
> a profound effect on your chance for survival."

❖ *Do you know where you are?*

Choose Your Own Team

At Daniel's request, the king appointed Shadrach, Meshach, and Abednego to be in charge of all the affairs of the province of Babylon. *DANIEL 2:49*

The company's new president had been highly recruited by the chairman of the board, who proudly told a stockholder gathering, "Caroline Menicco [not her real name] is going to stand this company up and get it running again."

Unfortunately, the board told Caroline to keep a couple of people on the executive team whom she saw as part of the problem. The old guard fought her every initiative, and the turnaround failed. The company was dissolved, and Caroline's promising career was permanently tarnished.

Daniel asked the king to appoint his countrymen in key positions, and Nebuchadnezzar wisely realized that leaders need people around them in whom they can confide.

New leaders can take your organization in exciting new directions. When you bring in new talent, give them freedom to survey the landscape and make changes where they are needed.

❖ *Current staff shouldn't be eliminated without cause; neither should they be passed along as part of the furniture.*

Keep Your Promises

Joshua said to the two spies, "Keep your promise. Go to the prostitute's house and bring her out, along with all her family." *JOSHUA 6:22*

Rahab was a prostitute in Jericho. For unknown reasons, she protected the two spies Joshua sent to gather intelligence about the city's defenses. When the Israelites blew their horns and "the walls came a-tumblin' down," Joshua honored the commitment his men had made to protect her.

It is easy to forget the little guy in the heat of battle.

Promises made to a small supplier often fall prey to rapid growth or competitive pressures. Special arrangements with a customer come under intense scrutiny when you outgrow the need to protect every relationship.

It would have been easy for Joshua to break the promise to Rahab, but he didn't, and God included this story in his book.

The leadership lesson is very clear. Honor your commitments, regardless of the cost or the rationale for doing otherwise.

❖ *God does what he says he'll do. You should too.*

Equip Yourself for Good Works

All Scripture is inspired by God. . . . God uses it to prepare and equip his people to do every good work.   *2 TIMOTHY 3:16-17*

God really wants you to succeed in your professional life, and he inspired writers over a span of 1,500 years to provide you with comprehensive guidelines for doing so.

Between Genesis and Revelation, you'll find examples and lessons that can equip you for every good work.

Paul wasn't just speaking to people with full-time Christian vocations. It isn't just pastors, teachers, missionaries, and clerks in Christian bookstores who are equipped—God's assistance is there for *all* God's people:

accountants, bricklayers, concert pianists, dermatologists, electricians, football players, gardeners, housepainters, illusionists, judges, kite makers, lawyers, martial artists, night watchmen, oil changers, pilots, quality-control experts, reporters, short-order cooks, telephone operators, union bosses, veterinarians, watchmakers, X-ray techs, yarmulke sewers, and zookeepers.

❖ *You are God's unique creation. His book was written with you in mind.*

See People in Person

[Paul] said good-bye and left for Macedonia. While there, he encouraged the believers in all the towns he passed through. Then he traveled down to Greece, where he stayed for three months . . . [while] preparing to sail back to Syria. *ACTS 20:1-3*

Ah, technology.

Using the Internet, I can arrange a video conference with people in six different time zones. We can share files, draw on each other's screens, and have a transcriptionist provide notes for everyone within hours of the meeting's end.

Paul was an effective communicator. His letters were first-century blogs and podcasts. His messengers were human MP3 files and QuickTime movies.

Paul also understood the value of being face-to-face with people.

Nothing can replace shaking people's hands, sitting across the table from them, sharing a meal, or sitting in their offices and looking out their windows.

Whether your organization stretches around the globe or across the hall, get up from your chair and visit the people you are leading.

❖ *Make a list of all the people you will visit today.*

Monitor Staff Morale

This is what Pharaoh says: I will not provide any more straw for you. Go and get it yourselves. Find it wherever you can. But you must produce just as many bricks as before! *EXODUS 5:10-11*

The office manager stands in front of her staff, saying, "Management has decided they can't afford to fill our two openings. With things as tight as they are, we're not allowed any more overtime, even during the software upgrade scheduled for next week."

Go back and read the verse from Exodus. From a staff-morale perspective, there's no difference between the modern version and the one from ancient Egypt.

You might argue that the motives are different, but motives don't mean much when workers are pushed to their limits through no fault of their own.

Have your goals outgrown the organization's ability to achieve them? Is it time to take careful inventory of staff morale?

❖ *You're the leader. Where are you leading them?*

Accept Honors Graciously

Joseph took charge of the entire land of
Egypt. *GENESIS 41:45*

It's confession time.

A few years ago, the leaders at our church asked
me to join the elder board. This was an honor, as
the men who had served previously were among the
most godly and wise people I have ever known.

I had reservations about my qualifications. Once
these were addressed, the proper thing to do was to
accept or decline the appointment. Instead, I dishon-
ored the people who had asked me to serve by joking
that they had scraped the bottom of the barrel. I said
I would serve until they came to their senses and
asked me to leave.

What a jerk.

Compare this to how Joseph accepted the honor
bestowed by Pharaoh.

Joseph did not question the appointment or hem
and haw about whether he was qualified for the job.

This thirty-year-old former slave and prison
inmate gracefully accepted his good fortune and
honored his benefactor by humbly setting about the
job at hand.

A class act.

❖ *Are you more like Joseph, or more like me?*

Deliver Bad News Respectfully

All the living things on earth died. . . . God wiped out every living thing on the earth. *GENESIS 7:21-23*

This was a gruesome picture. The whole earth was covered with water. This was Katrina, Rita, and the Sri Lanka tsunami rolled into one and spread across the entire planet. There's no way to put sugar sprinkles on the news or spin it into something it wasn't. This was bad news, plain and simple.

As leaders, we are sometimes required to deliver bad news. There is no substitute for simply explaining the facts without hyperbole, doublespeak, or cow manure.

When your announcement will affect people's lives or livelihoods, you owe them the respect of letting them decide what spin to put on the situation.

A pig with lipstick is still a pig.

❖ *It surely broke God's heart to see the devastation of the flood, but he couldn't hide from the tough decision. When it's your turn to do the same, be compassionate, fair, and honest.*

Ask God for Wisdom

If you need wisdom, ask our generous God, and he
will give it to you. *JAMES 1:5*

Some questions don't have right or wrong answers:

Coke or Pepsi? Paper or plastic? Mac or PC?

We don't get hung up on simple questions because
the consequences of our choices are pretty small.

However, some questions can tie us in knots for
days:

- Which of these two great applicants should I hire?
- I've been accepted at two outstanding schools.
    Which should I choose?
- Should I take the new job, or stay here and take
    the promotion?

Deciding between two or more right answers is what
wisdom and discernment are all about, and going to
God with your dilemma can help you make a final
choice.

Are you stuck on the horns of a dilemma right
now? James promises that God will not rebuke you
for seeking his guidance. Go to God, ask for wisdom,
and then make your choice.

❖ *It is not a sign of weakness to ask the
Creator of the universe for advice.*

Give God Your Worries

Give all your worries and cares to God, for he cares about you.   *1 PETER 5:7*

Leaders have a lot to worry about.

People are counting on you to make the right decisions.

Folks say it's lonely at the top and often it is. But how can you be lonely with all those people looking to you to make the right move?

In the introduction to his wonderful book *Leadership Prayers*, Richard Kriegbaum speaks of a leader's relationship to God:

> "Leaders do not pray to inform God of what is happening. He already knows. And they do not pray to get him to do what they want. He already wants what is best for everyone involved."[1]

What I read between Richard Kriegbaum's lines is that God is aching for you to bring him your worries. He knows what's on your mind and in your heart, and he has cleared his appointment calendar to spend quality one-on-one time with you.

❖ *God inspired Peter to include these words in his letter. Now he wants you to take him at his word.*

[1] Richard Kriegbaum, *Leadership Prayers* (Wheaton, IL: Tyndale, 1998), vii.

Communicate Your Intentions

Then God said, "Let us make human beings in our image." *GENESIS 1:26*

My wife and I enjoy second-row seats for our local symphony orchestra's six-concert series. Sitting this close to the front, we can hear the conductor speak to the players between selections. We can also see his facial expressions during the performance—it's quite clear that he uses more than just his hands to communicate with the fifty-some musicians before him.

We've noticed a particular connection between the maestro and his concertmistress, the first-chair violinist. They exchange brief comments at the beginning of the evening and often make eye contact during a performance.

The conductor is clearly the person in charge, but he could never complete his task without communicating his plans to those around him.

"Let *us* make human beings . . ." (emphasis added).

❖ *As the leader, you are in charge and the decision is yours to make, but—just as God did—it is vitally important that you keep your key people in the loop.*

Apply Change Buffers

Fill a two-quart container with manna to preserve it for your descendants. Then later generations will be able to see the food I gave you in the wilderness.   *EXODUS 16:32*

In his blockbuster book *Future Shock,* Alvin Toffler observes the rapidly accelerating pace of change in the 1970s and suggests that one way to mitigate the damage of such upheaval is to apply "change buffers."

Change buffers remind us that some things will never change, thus providing stability and relief.

Perhaps your organization is experiencing a period of rough water. Maybe a lot of change is happening, and folks feel as if they are wandering in the wilderness.

You can buffer them against the ravaging effects of too much change by recalling stories from the company's past. Show them that the water will eventually become smooth again.

The preserved manna gave the Israelites hope for the future by reminding them of the past.

❖ *Whenever you introduce a dramatic change, provide a buffer by also emphasizing the things that will not change.*

Be Fruitful As You Multiply

The Holy Spirit produces this kind of fruit in our lives: love, joy, peace, patience, kindness, goodness, faithfulness, gentleness, and self-control. *GALATIANS 5:22-23*

Our little company was growing by leaps and bounds. We were unstoppable. Goals were achieved and new objectives were set.

Look out, future—here we come.

When you drive fast, it's best to look far down the road so you can anticipate whatever might stand in the way. In doing so, you tend to lose sight of what's close at hand.

We had unknowingly run over some of our employees by not treating them with the respect they deserved. We hadn't listened to their concerns.

Our CEO realized this and challenged the leadership team to study this passage in Galatians. He encouraged each of us to "produce a bumper crop of fruit" in our relationships with the staff.

I spend a lot of time in front of the computer, so I typed each of the words into my screen-saver program and was constantly reminded of my need to grow healthy fruit.

❖ *Be fruitful as you multiply.*

Stay in the Driver's Seat

We hear that some of you are living idle lives, refusing to work and meddling in other people's business. *2 THESSALONIANS 3:11*

Have you ever been a passenger on a road that
you typically drive down yourself? Riding in the
passenger's seat allows you to see things that you
normally miss because your eyes are on the road.
When you drive, you don't have the luxury of
looking at the scenery.

The same applies to work situations. Employees
who don't have enough to do may go sightseeing and
stick their noses where they don't belong.

Paul encourages these meddlers to "settle down
and work" (2 Thessalonians 3:12). It is a leader's
responsibility to help them do so.

It's tempting to ignore busybodies, but allowing
them to continue meddling compounds the problem.
They don't do their own work, and they prevent others from doing theirs.

Call the idlers aside and ask them if they have
enough work to do. Thank them for their interest in
other assignments, and clearly encourage them to pay
attention to their own tasks.

❖ *You need drivers, not passengers.*

Remember Your History

Remember, these instructions are a permanent law that you and your descendants must observe forever. When you enter the land the LORD has promised to give you, you will continue to observe this ceremony. *EXODUS 12:24-25*

Every year at the company Christmas party, the founder and president stands up, clears his throat, fidgets nervously, and tells the story of how he and his brother started out with one delivery wagon and about ten dollars between them.

At another firm, the HR director schedules a lunch with the boss for all new hires. Each person has a one-on-one chat with the founder and hears how the place started on a dream and a prayer.

Remembering the journey helps to answer questions about why things are done the way they are.

Knowing how you got where you are can help you see where you're going.

Does your organization celebrate relevant traditions? Find the longest tenured member of the team and ask them how the organization got to where it is today.

❖ *Successful futures are built on foundations laid in the past.*

Speak to People's Hearts

Gideon replied, "What have I accomplished com-
pared to you?" . . . When the men of Ephraim heard
Gideon's answer, their anger subsided.
JUDGES 8:2-3

Daryl Travis is a marketing-science expert at
Brand-Trust in Chicago. He studies how our brains
process advertising messages and has concluded that
emotions play a much greater role in our responses to
advertising than we would care to admit.

Gideon had just come back from a decisive victory
over the Midianites, and the men of Ephraim were
upset because they weren't invited to participate in
the battle.

Instead of running through the logical reasons
why he had not chosen them to fight, Gideon
calmed their fears and made them feel important. He
appealed to their hearts.

Emotion instead of analysis.

We are often tempted to focus on the facts, forgetting how those facts might make someone feel. A
more effective approach is to get the facts straight,
then look for a way to deliver them that appeals to
the heart rather than the head.

❖ *How do you make people feel?*

Know Your People's Hearts

Then he asked them, "But who do you say I am?"   *MATTHEW 16:15*

This is part of a classic exchange between Jesus and Peter. After this conversation, Jesus named Peter to a special leadership position and gave him "the keys of the Kingdom of Heaven" (Matthew 16:19).

In reading the entire passage, it is clear that Jesus is looking for a very specific answer. I am convinced he already knew what Peter would say, so why did Jesus want Peter to answer the questions out loud?

There is great value in having someone look you in the eye and verbally affirm what you already know (or suspect) is in his or her heart.

There is also great danger in presuming that similar interests and experiences automatically confirm common beliefs or a shared vision.

It is important to know the hearts of the people you appoint to key leadership roles. Peter was apparently the only one who answered Jesus correctly.

❖ *Ask the tough questions and expect the right answers when you plan to give someone a key position on your team.*

Be Faithful in Small Things

If you are faithful in little things, you will be faithful in large ones.   *LUKE 16:10*

The temperature in a kiln reaches nearly two thousand degrees as green clay is transformed into a durable piece of pottery. Increasing the temperature too fast can cause dunting, which leaves tiny cracks that remain unnoticed until the piece falls apart under normal use.

Young leaders are sometimes forced into situations that dunt their spirits. As they take on more than they can handle, too many of them burn out and have a difficult time recovering. Their young families suffer, the organization suffers, and seeds of self-doubt are planted where they probably should not be.

Jesus provides two lessons in this passage. Most obvious is the imperative that one's ability must be proven before more responsibility is given.

Less obvious but nonetheless critical is the duty placed on experienced leaders to protect their progeny from too steep a trajectory. Don't set them up for failure by turning the heat up too fast.

❖ *Are the young leaders under your care being groomed for success or failure?*

Pace Your Growth

I will make all your enemies turn and run. . . . But
I will not drive them out in a single year, because
the land would become desolate. . . . I will drive
them out a little at a time until your population has
increased enough.   *EXODUS 23:27-30*

When the small advertising agency was started, there
were four employees. They were very effective, and
business began to fall from the sky. It was great.

After hiring a handful of support people and rent-
ing the necessary office gear for them, the staff was
shocked when the founder announced that they had
to start refusing new business.

"We have outgrown our cash flow, and if we want
to be around for the long haul, we need to postpone
some business until our infrastructure catches up
with our reality."

God had great plans for the Israelites, but he knew
they had to be phased in over time.

❖ *It may fly in the face of conventional wisdom,
but not all growth is good for your organization.
Make sure you are ready to grow before you
fertilize your ideas.*

Pay Attention to the Future

I will hide you in the crevice of the rock and cover you with my hand until I have passed by. Then I will remove my hand and let you see me from behind. But my face will not be seen.   *EXODUS 33:22-23*

This dialogue between Moses and Yahweh shows us another of God's leadership attributes:

God's focus is always on the future.

Reggie McNeal tells it this way: "After all these years of talking to bushes, clouds and pillars of fire, Moses asks God if he can see his face. God says that wouldn't be such a good idea, but he compromises by letting Moses see his back, after he's passed by. . . .

Perhaps the reason we only see God's back is that he is always facing where we haven't been. He is always leading. Always out front. Never looking back."[1]

❖ *Learn from the past.*

❖ *Live in the present.*

❖ *Pay attention to the future—because that's where God is.*

---

[1] Dr. Reggie McNeal, The Present Future seminar, Walnut Creek, California, November 2005.

Establish Clear Boundaries

You may freely eat the fruit of every tree in the garden—except the tree of the knowledge of good and
evil. *GENESIS 2:16-17*

Imagine a tennis court with no lines or boundaries.
Every shot is "in," and serves never land in the wrong
court. The game would be much easier to play—
wouldn't it?

Without lines, both players would run around the
court like a couple of Monty Python characters until
one of them gave up or dropped from exhaustion.
Those exciting over-the-shoulder backhands that
just barely catch an outside corner wouldn't mean a
thing, and guys like John McEnroe would need to
find a different way of gaining fame.

Boundaries make tennis work.

Knowing where the lines are and learning to play
the game inside them is what sets great players apart
from weekend wannabes.

God told Adam he could "freely eat" within the
parameters he had established.

❖ *Do people in your game know where the
boundaries are? More importantly—have you
given them the freedom to do what they do best
inside the lines?*

Start Over When Necessary

The Israelites were in great distress. Finally, they cried out to the LORD for help, saying, "We have sinned against you. . . . Punish us as you see fit, only rescue us today from our enemies." Then the Israelites put aside their foreign gods and served the LORD.   *JUDGES 10:9-10, 15-16*

My assignment was to fix the annual sales conference. Most people only showed up because it was required, and few left having gained much by attending. The format had been tweaked every year for the past decade. It was now a hodgepodge of elements that ran behind schedule. Half the seats were empty by the second day.

I decided to "blow it up."

We changed everything, including the seating arrangements and starting time. We scratched all the old ideas and started over.

It worked. Nearly every seat was occupied when we concluded, early, on the second day.

Israel was in great distress. They needed to blow up their old and start over. Minor adjustments would no longer do the trick.

❖ *You should not take such drastic steps lightly, but they must be part of your repertoire for moving forward.*

Stay on Track

They have abandoned me—the fountain of living water. And they have dug for themselves cracked cisterns that can hold no water at all!
JEREMIAH 2:13

Keeping your eyes on the mission is critical for two reasons:

+ Losing focus slows your momentum and puts the objective that much further away.
+ At the same time, you become distracted by something else and actually head off in the wrong direction.

This is double trouble. You've not only stopped moving toward the objective, but you've veered off course and will need to use resources to get back on track.

The Israelites were no longer focused on their mission of serving God. They had gone beyond ignoring him to actually worshiping other gods. The consequences were dire.

Staying on course isn't always easy. When shiny new ideas vie for your attention, stop and ask, *How will this help us reach our goal? How does this fit into our mission?*

❖ *If you can't answer the question or the answer doesn't feel right, put the idea on the shelf and turn your attention back to the future you are committed to achieving.*

Individually Bless Your Staff

These are the twelve tribes of Israel, and this is what their father said as he told his sons good-bye. He blessed each one with an appropriate message.   *GENESIS 49:28*

Reuben was unruly. Simeon and Levi were violent. Judah was a young lion. Zebulun would live by the sea. Issachar was sturdy. Dan was a governor. Gad would be a victim. Asher would produce food for kings. Naphtali was a free spirit. Joseph was the foal of a wild donkey. Benjamin was a ravenous wolf.

Jacob knew the personalities of his twelve sons and wove a special blessing around each man's unique qualities. If one son showed an aptitude for fishing, it wouldn't make sense to bless him with rich farmland.

Understanding the unique abilities of those who report directly to you and blessing them with assignments to match their personalities can dramatically increase your effectiveness as a leader.

❖ *Everyone on your team excels at something. Help them determine what that is, and put it to good use to further your agenda.*

Don't Create Double Trouble

No one can serve two masters. . . . You will be
devoted to one and despise the other.
MATTHEW 6:24

It always sounds like such a smart way to stretch
payroll dollars.

Bill and Janice both have executive assistants. Bill's
assistant retires, and rather than hire a replacement,
they decide to share Janice's assistant, Shirley.

Bill and Janice have different management styles.
She's an early riser who hands out assignments in
advance of their due date. He stays late every night
and works on very tight deadlines.

Shirley is being asked to serve two masters.

Jesus couldn't have been any clearer—you can't
do that! Yet Bill and Janice have put Shirley in the
impossible position of having to do so.

You may have good intentions, but the shared
positions you create require those employees to make
difficult decisions they shouldn't have to make.

❖ *Arrange the situation so that the shared
employee only reports to one person. One solution may be an office manager who coordinates
assignments from multiple bosses.*

Welcome New Talent

So now we must choose a replacement for Judas. *ACTS 1:21*

The senior pastor had been with the church for eight years. Weekly attendance had grown from 350 to 1,500. Things were humming along nicely—and then he took a position at another church.

Many in the congregation thought he was irreplaceable, but the new pastor was better suited to maintaining a healthy organization. The church's needs had changed, so the talent pool also needed to change.

Vacancies are opportunities to make critical adjustments in your team's core competencies.

Judas had played an important role in the ministry by handling the money. Until the time of his betrayal, he was a trusted player.

The disciples didn't dwell on the past. They looked to the future and chose a replacement with the qualities needed to further their mission. Their needs had changed, so they looked for someone more suited to evangelism than financial management.

❖ *An opening on your team is a gift from God. He's giving you the opportunity to make changes and get ready for the future.*

Pay It Forward

Encourage each other and build each other up.
1 THESSALONIANS 5:11

In her novel *Pay It Forward*, Catherine Ryan Hyde explores the potential effect of a young boy who does good deeds for people and asks them to repay his kindness by doing similar good deeds for three other people.

The boy's kindness is multiplied exponentially across the country as millions of people go out of their way to encourage each other in the way that Paul urged the Thessalonian church to do.

The book became a movie, and the country fell in love with Trevor McKinney because what he did was so unusual.

Why is it so much easier to criticize than to encourage?

As a leader, you are in a position to make a difference in the lives of people who have been placed in your care.

Imagine the effect you might have on your organization if you make a concentrated effort to follow Paul's advice.

Pay It Forward was fiction. Paul's writing was inspired by God.

❖ *Give it a try. I know you can do it.*

Utilize Your Senior Employees

When the queen mother heard what was happening, she hurried to the banquet hall.   *DANIEL 5:10*

The recollections of your senior employees are among your organization's most valuable assets. Their stories of early days can provide a foundation for recent employees who wonder why you do things as you do, or how you got to where you are today.

Belshazzar had assumed Nebuchadnezzar's throne, but he hadn't maintained his father's relationship with Daniel. When handwriting appeared on the wall of Belshazzar's banquet hall, he was frightened, and the whole palace was atwitter, wondering what it meant.

Nebuchadnezzar's wife heard about the situation and rushed in to tell her son about Daniel's ability to interpret dreams. Daniel was summoned and revealed the message's meaning.

Longtime employees sometimes resist change or may not share your enthusiasm for the future, but they can help you avoid costly errors by recalling previous mistakes. Their input can speed a project along by their suggestions of contacts or shortcuts developed on earlier jobs.

❖ *Do you have a team of trusted senior advisors?*

Don't Be Arrogant

Their arrogance testifies against them.   *HOSEA 7:10*

My dictionary defines *arrogance* as "having disregard for other people."

God has many things to say against arrogant people. He holds all of us in such high regard that anyone who doesn't hold others in high regard is operating counter to his ideals.

I don't believe that anyone sets out to be arrogant. No one says,

"I'm just not conceited enough" or "My goal is to belittle twice as many people today."

We become arrogant through the force of our self-perspective.

"I'm the boss; my opinions matter more."
"I'm older."
"I'm richer."
"She's just a waitress."

❖ *Make it a point today to hold everyone you see in higher regard than you normally would. Go out of your way to think more highly of them than you do of yourself. Then reflect back on how much different your day has been as it draws to a close.*

Manage God's Resources Well

Everything comes from him and exists by his power and is intended for his glory.   ROMANS 11:36

"Thank you for the vote of confidence in our agency, Ms. Thompson. You can be sure we will treat the money you've entrusted to us as if it were our very own."

No, thanks.

If I'm going to hire an agency to handle my money, I want them to treat it as if it were mine, because it is. Their job is to put themselves in my shoes and do what I would do in every situation. They are certainly more skilled in their specialty, but their results should support my goals, not theirs.

You are God's agent. Everything you have is his.

Your time is his time. Your past is really his past. Your money and your ideas are his. Your future is his gift to you.

When you hire an agency, you expect them to understand your goals and manage your assets accordingly.

God's objectives are for you to glorify him by loving others.

❖ *Are you looking forward to your next performance review?*

Do What You Say You Will Do

God will do this, for he is faithful to do what he says. *1 CORINTHIANS 1:9*

The fund-raising department of a large private university waited anxiously for word on the selection of a new director.

When the final choice was announced, the team was excited. Although no one in the department had ever worked with the new director, she had a reputation for following through on her commitments. Many references mentioned a plaque that hung on her office wall, which said,

> *I will do*
> *what I say*
> *I will do*

Leading involves taking people to places they haven't been, showing them things they've never seen, and encouraging them to do things they have never done.

It's easier to get people out of their comfort zones if they trust that you can deliver the goods. Paul reminded the church in Corinth that God had been faithful, to them and their ancestors, for thousands of years.

Your team needs a leader they can trust to be there when the vision gets blurry and goals seem out of reach.

❖ *Are you that leader?*

Motivate Others to Good Works

Let us think of ways to motivate one another to acts of love and good works.   *HEBREWS 10:24*

The company was tremendously profitable, yet the amount budgeted for charitable contributions seemed paltry compared to our bottom line. Leaders wanted to do more but couldn't decide where the money should go.

Someone had the idea of starting a contest among the various departments to see which of them could do the most good with a sizeable sum placed under their control.

The departments were told, "Take this money and do something good with it, locally or globally. The decision is yours. We'd like you to share regular updates, and at the end of the year, we will all vote on whose project was most successful."

The results were amazing. Each department adopted a different cause and dedicated their efforts to "acts of love and good works." Employee morale was at an all-time high, and it was a better place to work.

❖ *Do you put your money where your heart is? Perhaps you can add "acts of love and good works" to the standards against which you measure your organization's success.*

Be Generous

There was an abundance of royal wine, reflecting the king's generosity. By edict of the king, no limits were placed on the drinking. *ESTHER 1:7-8*

Ebenezer Scrooge has been a popular character for a couple of centuries because generosity—or its absence—is such a powerful force.

Was the world's favorite "lousy boss" really such a bad guy? Despite his villainous portrayal, wasn't Scrooge simply being careful with his money—frugal, cautious, prudent, and thrifty?

Or does the world despise him because he replaced stewardship with stinginess?

Just like Scrooge, Xerxes had every right to keep what was his. But he chose to share it without limit. The guest list for his celebration included everyone in the kingdom. There is no evidence that people were required to meet certain performance standards to benefit from his largesse.

Are you more like Scrooge or Xerxes? Do you lay aside what's rightfully yours to help others achieve their goals?

❖ *Is there someone who would benefit, right now, from your generosity?*

Don't Be a Loner

It is not good for the man to be alone.
GENESIS 2:18

As the leader of your organization, you have a unique perspective, because the buck always stops with you. Everyone is looking to you for vision and direction.

God placed Adam in the Garden to watch over it, and despite all the confidence he had in Adam, God knew the man needed someone to confide in.

Close relationships are extremely valuable for people in leadership positions. Having a handful of people you trust for confidential advice can make the difference between a good decision and a great one. Having a close friend who always speaks the truth will save you from making costly mistakes in judgment.

Take a moment right now to inventory your relationships. You should be able to count on one hand the number of people who are members of your inner circle and with whom you share mutual knowledge and respect.

❖ *There are many reasons why it is not good for you to be alone. Make sure you aren't.*

Protect Your Image

I will not take so much as a single thread or san-
dal thong from what belongs to you. Otherwise
you might say, "I am the one who made Abram
rich." *GENESIS 14:23*

You can have the purest motives, but if your actions
are misunderstood, you might as well have stolen
candy from little children, because perception is what
matters.

Image management has gotten a bad rap because
spin doctors weave straw into fool's gold and often
try to make us believe what isn't true, but there's real
value in protecting your image from misinterpretation.

Your organization's image is a valuable asset. It
doesn't show up on the ledger, and you can't borrow
against its equity, but losing it can do more damage than a fire in your warehouse or a virus in your
computer network.

As a leader, you should assign someone the specific
job of proactively protecting your company's image.
Don't wait for rumors to start—by then it's too late.

❖ *However you decide to handle it, remember
that image is vital.*

Put Your Money Where Your Heart Is

Wherever your treasure is, there the desires of your heart will also be.   *MATTHEW 6:21*

If you want to know what's really important to an organization, don't read their mission statement—spend an hour looking at their budget and their fiscal policies.

Does the organization talk about the importance of strong family relationships? The budget should allow them to hire enough people so that workers (including executives) can spend adequate time away from the job.

How do they decide on the price for something? Do they ask, "How much can we charge?" or "What's the lowest possible price we can afford to set?"

Do they claim, "People are our most important asset"? Look at the wage scale. Is it the highest or the lowest for their area and industry?

Fiscal responsibility is not the issue. That's a given. There's a more serious question to ask.

❖ *Are you putting your money where your heart is?*

Show Respect, Regardless

The LORD God called to the man, "Where are you?" *GENESIS 3:9*

In the dialog that followed Adam's first sin, God demonstrated a leadership attribute that is very difficult for us to imitate.

Obviously, God knew the answers to his own questions, but rather than directly accuse Adam, he asked questions and followed Adam's lead in the conversation.

Despite the dire consequence of Adam's actions, God honored him by allowing him his day in court. God would have been justified in sweeping his hand over Eden and wiping Adam off the face of the earth, but he gave Adam a chance to explain himself.

Let's be crystal clear—his first sin was a monumental mistake on Adam's part. His actions forever changed the relationship between God and his Creation. Even so, God showed an incredible level of respect for Adam in his approach.

❖ *As leaders, we sometimes put the agenda ahead of the people we've been given to lead. No matter what they do, and despite the seriousness of their actions, we should show them the same respect that God granted Adam in the Garden.*

Recall Your Burning Bush

When the LORD saw Moses coming to take a closer look, God called to him from the middle of the bush, "Moses! Moses!"   *EXODUS 3:4*

My pastor has a great way of encouraging his elder board to make tough decisions. "There's a time," he says, "when elders just need to be elders."

You owe it to the people who follow you to step up and do the job you were called to do.

For Moses, it all started at the bush. He tried to convince God to pick someone else, but in the end he accepted the mantle of leadership and changed the world.

Leaders have a responsibility to lead, and until they exercise their "burning bush authority" to do so, they aren't really doing so.

Is there a similar incident in your history? Do you have a burning bush story to tell?

❖ *I wonder if Moses ever sat alone in his tent and thought about the burning bush. If he did, it must have given him new energy for the difficult events of his life.*

Question "Obvious" Successions

As Samuel grew old, he appointed his sons to be judges over Israel. Joel and Abijah . . . were not like their father, for they were greedy for money. They accepted bribes and perverted justice.

1 SAMUEL 8:1-3

Every opening on your leadership team should be subject to review, especially if an apparent successor has been with your organization for a long time.

In Samuel's case, the obvious reason for hiring from outside was his sons' corruption. But there's another reason to conduct a thorough search when you need to fill a key leadership role.

Filling a leadership opening with someone who has been around for a long time could mean missing a chance to bring new ideas into the organization.

Loyalty is a good thing, unless it's loyalty to the way you've always done things.

New people also bring an exciting sense of uncertainty and anticipation to the table that causes everyone to think differently, and this is almost always a good thing.

❖ *Succession to leadership should never be automatic or guaranteed.*

Expect Team Members to Contribute

Anyone who isn't with me opposes me, and anyone who isn't working with me is actually working against me. MATTHEW 12:30

In the sport of dogsled racing, the musher (driver) must keep watch over the condition of each dog. If one goes lame, the entire team is slowed down.

The lame dog doesn't intentionally hold the team back, but seven healthy dogs can run faster than seven healthy dogs plus one lame dog in the harness. By not running up to speed, one lame animal actually works against the others.

Leadership teams are like this. A single member who never quite gets with the program compromises the group's effectiveness. Such people do more damage by staying on the team than they do by leaving.

Jesus had harsh words for people who pretend to be on a team but don't contribute toward its objectives.

Objections and disagreements should be encouraged, but once decisions are made and the team begins to move forward, it's time to fall into line and support the team effort.

❖ *Anything else is counterproductive.*

Get People Talking

The woman was convinced . . . so she took some of the fruit and ate it. Then she gave some to her husband. *GENESIS 3:6*

In his book *The Tipping Point,* Malcolm Gladwell introduces the concept of Connectors. He describes these people as passing ideas along very effective informal channels of communication.

Planting ideas with key individuals who will share your message with others can start a chain reaction that is more effective than any type of traditional advertising or marketing campaign.

The serpent looked for someone who was open to his message. He planted the seed and waited for the word-of-mouth process to work. The serpent didn't ask Eve to share the message with anyone. She was convinced, and that was all it took to change the course of history.

❖ *People are more likely to believe your story if it comes from an acquaintance, so to spread your idea, get people talking to each other.*

Consider Strategic Partnerships

The men of Judah said to their relatives from the tribe of Simeon, "Join with us to fight against the Canaanites living in the territory allotted to us." *JUDGES 1:3*

The objective in basketball is to score more points than the other team. The scoreboard logs how well each team did during the allotted time, but players are also recognized for the number of times they assist another player to score points.

Every player has individual objectives, such as the desire to be on a Wheaties box, but the team works together to achieve common goals. They form a strategic alliance.

The tribes of Judah and Simeon had similar goals. They also wanted to preserve their distinctiveness, so they formed an alliance. Each tribe contributed its own competencies and resources.

Strategic alliances tend to succeed when both sides clearly understand the other's reasons for participating, so be candid about your goals from the outset.

❖ *Perhaps you have a big project looming that would benefit from a partnership with someone who shares a similar goal. You may not need to fight the battle alone.*

Produce Good Fruit

Yes, just as you can identify a tree by its fruit, so you can identify people by their actions.

MATTHEW 7:20

We all have an image and an identity.

Identity is how we see ourselves in the mirror. Image is how others see us. It's best to keep these two closely aligned. You want people to see the same thing in you that you see in the mirror.

Jesus understood the value of a good image, and he tells us that there's no way to fake it.

You can't trick people into thinking you're wise if you do foolish things. It's impossible to convince the board of directors you're able to make smart choices if you're always making mistakes.

Do people think you're always late for meetings? Try getting there on time. If you want them to respect your ideas, say something intelligent.

People will forgive an occasional bad day, but if you sense a pattern in their responses, it's probably caused by some persistant behavior on your part.

❖ *Sometimes people have a bad hair day, but usually they just have lousy haircuts.*

Know How to Recharge

Before daybreak the next morning, Jesus got up
and went out to an isolated place to pray.
MARK 1:35

Some of us are introverts and some of us are
extroverts. We have many other qualities, but we all
fit into one of these two categories. Being one or the
other has little to do with being shy or outgoing. It
pertains to how we recharge our emotional batteries.

People are often surprised to learn that I'm a raging introvert. After leading a large group discussion,
I am emotionally drained and need some time alone
to recharge. I like people, but I get my strength from
solitude.

Perhaps you're an extrovert who draws energy from
being with others. It's important to know which
works for you, so you can schedule solitude or social
time into your day.

Jesus found time to be alone. He was not anti-
social, although his wanting to be alone may have
raised a few eyebrows in his day.

❖ Who did he think he was, going off by himself all the time?

Ask Good Questions

[Jesus] turned to his critics and asked, "Does the law permit good deeds on the Sabbath, or is it a day for doing evil? Is this a day to save life or to destroy it?"   *MARK 3:4*

Comedian Bob Newhart built a career on his ability to stage rib-tickling, one-way conversations that often involved the answers to hilarious questions.

Cast members at Disney theme parks are trained to respond to guest questions with questions of their own, to make sure the answer they give is what the customer really wanted to know.

As a talk-show host, I learned that asking good questions was the secret to getting good answers from my guests.

Jesus was a master at asking questions.

Who do men say that I am?

Where is your husband?

How can Satan cast out Satan?

His questions weren't meant to confuse or obfuscate an issue, but to help people think more clearly about something.

❖ *Leaders are often tempted to provide instant answers. Perhaps you need to slow down and learn to ask a few good questions. You may find the answers exciting.*

Remember God's Promises

The people of Israel . . . panicked when they saw the Egyptians overtaking them. They cried out to the LORD, and they said to Moses, "Why did you bring us out here to die in the wilderness?"
EXODUS 14:10-11

Don't you just want to scream? How quickly these people forgot who was in charge! Wasn't it just the day before that God's pillar of cloud was in front of them?

Oh wait—it's still there. What gives?

People lose sight of the vision very quickly, and you can't let this surprise you or get you offtrack.

Moses didn't skip a beat. He just repeated the promise, "Stay calm. The Lord himself will fight for you."

Human beings are predictable creatures. You can count on them to react the same way in similar situations, so you can pretty well guess when someone is going to lose sight of the vision.

❖ *Take a cue from Moses and stick with the plan. A calm and controlled response to their panic will do wonders for their perception of you as a leader who is in charge and worthy of following.*

Set a Good Example

Both Abraham and his son, Ishmael, were circumcised on that same day, along with all the other men and boys of the household. *GENESIS 17:26-27*

One of a leader's most difficult responsibilities is to set an example for the troops. It's easy to find reasons for ignoring certain guidelines, but doing so undermines your team-building efforts and erodes common objectives.

Consider the message you broadcast to the staff when you're the only one who doesn't wear the corporate uniform at a trade show.

Being on time for meetings, returning phone calls, and submitting expense vouchers on deadline are commonly abused. So are getting enough rest and taking vacations.

As a leader, sometimes you will do things no one else is doing. This defines the job, just like setting an example for others to follow. Abraham could have used a number of excuses to pull rank and avoid the inconvenience of circumcision.

❖ *Welcome to the tightrope. When in doubt, err on the side of being a team player.*

Value No-Holds-Barred Sessions

Surely you wouldn't do that! Should not the Judge of all the earth do what is right?   GENESIS 18:25

Wow! That was Abraham talking to God after being told that Sodom and Gomorrah would be consumed by fire. You and I know the story's outcome, but Abraham didn't, and I'm struck by his boldness.

There is also a valuable leadership lesson in God's calm response to Abraham's approach.

Good leaders allow key people to speak freely without fear of reprisal.

In a former position, I prearranged with my boss that I would reserve such conversations until we were alone. I always prefaced my comments with, "Mr. President." When he heard me say that, he knew I was heading into sensitive territory, and he honored me with his undivided attention.

Many leaders are isolated by the necessity of spending more time in the future than the present. These occasional no-holds-barred sessions can provide tremendous insight.

❖ *Are you the type of leader with whom people can speak freely? Don't answer too quickly.*

Eat in the Lunchroom

When the LORD had finished his conversation with Abraham, he went on his way, and Abraham returned to his tent. *GENESIS 18:33*

God and Abraham engaged in a conversation about the pending destruction of Sodom and Gomorrah. We know from the preceding verses that the dialog occurred during and after a meal in Abraham's tent.

The exchange strikes me as rather casual. When it concluded, there was no major pronouncement. God went on his way, and Abraham returned to whatever he was doing before the conversation began.

How long has it been since you brought your lunch to work and shared a table with people who work for you?

This can be tricky if it isn't done with the right attitude. You are invading their domain, so don't force an agenda. It's their lunch break, and your job is to listen.

❖ *They'll be a bit suspicious at first, but it will become more comfortable as time goes on. If you make it a regular practice, they'll even save room for you before they see you coming.*

Use Stories and Illustrations

Jesus used many similar stories and illustrations to teach the people as much as they could understand. In fact, in his public ministry he never taught without using parables. *MARK 4:33-34*

Sgt. Joe Friday is famous for his line, "Just the facts, ma'am. Just the facts." As the hard-nosed detective on the TV series *Dragnet,* Friday wasn't interested in the lady's involved story about what had happened. He only wanted to know what she had seen and heard.

That's not how most people are wired. We love stories.

The best way to sell people on an idea is to help them visualize the result. Do you want them to buy your shoes? Tell them how good their feet will feel. Are you running a political campaign? Help people imagine a better life with your candidate in office.

People make more donations to your camp scholarship fund when you tell them about a kid whose life was changed at camp.

Jesus didn't use PowerPoint or three-point sermons. He spoke in a way that people could relate to, and he shared stories that they could see themselves in.

❖ *Develop your ability to illustrate your points with stories.*

Censor Random Remarks

Then the king deeply regretted what he had said; but because of the vows he had made in front of his guests, he couldn't refuse her.   *MARK 6:26*

There are legendary stories about CEOs who wonder why their company has made a sweeping policy change. They discover that the change is the result of someone's overhearing a random comment they've made and interpreting it as a categorical directive.

Herod told his daughter she could have anything she wanted. She asked for something he didn't want to give her, but his authority couldn't be challenged even when it meant beheading someone he respected.

Leaders cultivate obedience as a necessary component of getting things done. When you signal a turn, you want your team to turn, and most of the time, this is a good thing.

Here's the caveat:

Your ability to steer the ship with a single command means that you can run it aground if your random comments are misinterpreted.

❖ *What you say in the elevator can become policy by tomorrow morning, so be careful what you say and where you say it.*

Add Some Exclamation Points!

Eve . . . became pregnant. When she gave birth to Cain, she said, "With the LORD's help, I have produced a man!"   *GENESIS 4:1*

Notice the exclamation point at the end of the sentence! Eve was excited. She had done something incredible, and she was shouting about it. If television had been around then, the cameras would have been rolling, and Eve would have been booked on *Oprah, Today,* and CNN. She was ecstatic.

Eve would probably not have been as excited had God crafted a baby boy from a handful of mud and given it to her. He could certainly have done so, but he let Eve experience the joy of doing what she was created to do.

You probably have more experience in your field than most of the people reporting to you, and it's often tempting to step in and take over a project. Doing so can easily ruin the spirit of the people who work hard to accomplish your objectives.

❖ *Look for ways to add exclamation points to the ends of your team's sentences.*

Establish Rapport

Then Moses and Aaron returned to Egypt and called all the elders of Israel together. Aaron told them everything the LORD had told Moses, and Moses performed the miraculous signs.

EXODUS 4:29-30

To put this in perspective, Moses had been gone for a long time, and he hadn't left Egypt on the best of terms (he had just killed an Egyptian). When he went back to solicit Hebrew support, he relied on someone from their community to make the initial introductions.

Aaron was a trusted member of the Jewish community who was obviously respected by the elders. He paved the way for Moses and asked the Egyptians to watch what his younger brother could do with a walking staff.

It's all about relationships. You can force people to do something without having established a relationship, but if you want to *lead* them, you'll need to build some rapport.

Since Moses and Aaron took time to establish a connection, "the people of Israel were convinced" (Exodus 4:31).

❖ *As a leader, you can't ask for more than that.*

Ask for Advice

The gardener answered, "Sir, give it one more chance. Leave it another year, and I'll give it special attention and plenty of fertilizer. If we get figs next year, fine. If not, then you can cut it down."

LUKE 13:8-9

Most of us are really good at just a couple of things. That's okay. God crafted each person to play certain roles, and he gave us unique sets of talents. I love knowing that I am not expected to know everything about everything.

The man in this parable planted a fig tree, and after three years it had still not produced any fruit. There's no indication of the man's occupation, but he must not have had a green thumb since he had a gardener.

"Cut it down," said the man. But with an expert's view of the situation, the gardener suggested different care and more fertilizer.

Asking the gardener's opinion probably saved a valuable asset that might have been sacrificed had the man relied on his own limited knowledge.

❖ *Admitting you need advice is a sign of wisdom. Don't hesitate to bring in experts.*

Avoid TMI

There is so much more I want to tell you, but you can't bear it now. *JOHN 16:12*

You have probably heard someone say during a conversation, "Oh, that's TMI."

It stands for "too much information" and is typically used when someone begins to share more details of a situation than anyone really wants to know.

"No need to describe the toe fungus, Bob. We get the picture."

We need a TMI alert buzzer for organizational communication. Too many leaders bury their staff and customers under superfluous detail that is unnecessary and overwhelming.

I've heard this referred to as the "fire hose syndrome." Someone asks for a glass of water, and they get drowned in a flood.

Jesus knew that his followers could only grasp so much at once, so he portioned out essential information at appropriate times.

If you blast folks with too much, they will have difficulty focusing on what really matters.

❖ *If people seem not to understand, perhaps you should give them less rather than more.*

Acknowledge Those Who Help You

The LORD has shown unfailing love and faithfulness to my master, for he has led me straight to my master's relatives. *GENESIS 24:27*

The next time you watch the *Academy Awards* on TV, keep a running tab of the winners who actually thank the people who helped them, as opposed to those who hog the spotlight by reciting a long list of names before the music starts and they're ushered offstage.

I get a kick out of the little guys and first-time winners who are genuinely grateful for the people who have helped them.

As a leader, you are often in a position to accept the help of others. You will reap tremendous benefits if you keep track of their assistance and find a way to thank them in public.

Abraham's servant was quick to acknowledge God's help in completing his mission.

❖ *When you offer genuine recognition of valuable aid, other people notice and give you points for your honesty and humanity.*

Improve Your Writing Skills

Because one person disobeyed God, many became sinners. But because one other person obeyed God, many will be made righteous.

ROMANS 5:19

In Romans 5:12-21, Paul presents the difference between Adam and Christ in an amazingly well-structured argument. Take a moment to read it. You'll be blown away by how thoroughly Paul covers the bases.

Paul exhibits strong communication skills as he conveys spiritual truth in this passage. His argument flows easily from one point to the next, he anticipates questions and answers them in context, and he leaves nothing unfinished.

I encourage you to pay more attention to the quality of your communication. Too many leaders take this for granted. Organizing your thoughts and writing well are important aspects of leadership that often take a backseat to the more urgent matters of budgets, operations, and problem solving.

Take a course in business writing. Have someone proofread your letters for clarity, grammar, and logic. Be critical of your arguments.

❖ *Great ideas won't go far if they're hidden behind a muddled line of reasoning.*

Have a Plan of Last Resort

I will wipe this human race I have created from the face of the earth. *GENESIS 6:7*

In the paragraph that precedes Noah's story, we see that things had gone terribly wrong with the world. When God surveyed the landscape, he saw that "everything . . . was consistently and totally evil" (Genesis 6:5).

Although the text doesn't say so, I believe God had tried reasoning with the people. We know that he is always looking for people through whom he can bless the world. Instead of using his incredible powers of persuasion, God took irreversible action.

The flood must have been a plan of last resort.

As a leader, you should be prepared to take drastic measures if there is no other way to save the mission. Sometimes incremental patches just aren't enough. In some situations, the problem lies too deep for anything but a flood.

❖ *Keep in mind that God used this tactic once in all of history. If you're considering a flood for your organization, seek God's personal advice in prayer. After all, he's already been through it.*

Choose Capable People

[Moses] chose capable men from all over Israel and appointed them as leaders over the people. . . . These men were always available to solve the people's common disputes. *EXODUS 18:25-26*

Moses was overwhelmed. He was the arbitrator for the entire population, and the task was consuming more time than he had available.

At the suggestion of his wife's father, Moses appointed men from each of the twelve tribes as regional managers for the organization. They provided the starting place for all decisions, and if there was something they couldn't handle, they brought it to Moses.

Leaders must set priorities for their own time. Those who don't often fall prey to well-intentioned subordinates who believe the boss wants to hear every little concern.

Do you really need to decide which coffeemaker to buy? Or whether the company should serve chicken or beef at the next annual picnic?

❖ *You have only a certain amount of time to do everything you're supposed to do. Don't waste it by making decisions that should be handled by your managers.*

Encourage New Ideas

We can rejoice, too, when we run into problems
and trials, for we know that they help us develop
endurance. *ROMANS 5:3*

How does your organization reward failure?

Intuit, the software giant that sells TurboTax and
Quicken, presents a "Swing for the Fence" award to
employees who come up with incredible ideas, even
if they fail.

Marketing people at Intuit say that the purpose of
the recognition is to "foster a culture of experimenta-
tion." By honoring big ideas regardless of their out-
comes, the company hopes to generate ideas that will
"change and improve the business."

Paul was writing to the Romans about spiritual
things, but God cares deeply about every aspect of
your life, including the time you spend using the
talents he's given you.

Most organizations try to avoid mistakes, but if
Paul is correct and mistakes make us stronger, perhaps we should let our guard down and swing for the
fence more often.

❖ *How long has it been since someone on
your team came in with a really crazy idea?*

Run with Purpose

So I run with purpose in every step. I am not just shadowboxing.   *1 CORINTHIANS 9:26*

Rick Warren's book, *The Purpose-Driven Life,* has sold a zillion copies worldwide because people are intrigued by the idea that their lives are more than a series of interconnected accidents; they *want* to have purpose, and *PDL* gives them a good starting place.

You have a mission statement hanging on a wall somewhere in the office. Most people in your organization know you have one, and a few of them can even recite it.

Does it give your employees purpose? Does it answer the question, How will what I am doing today make a difference?

Your mission statement should be short and concise. It should be the filter for your people's every activity. When they look at their to-do list for each day, they should be able to see how each task fills a purpose.

Paul had a laser-sharp focus on the reason for his existence. He ran everything through the simple filter of his mission.

❖ *Does your mission statement add clarity or confusion?*

Define Strategic Goals

So Esau swore an oath, thereby selling all his rights as the firstborn to his brother, Jacob.
GENESIS 25:33

If this isn't the ultimate example of desperation judgment, I don't know what is. Esau was on the verge of inheriting a huge fortune when he traded it away for a bowl of soup.

Decisions made in the heat of urgency are usually flawed.

As a leader, you need perspective on long-term solutions. The first line of defense against selling your future for a bowl of soup is to have well-defined strategic goals.

Understand where you are heading and what it takes to get there.

Having a good picture of the future can help you visualize the potential damage that desperate short-term decisions will cause.

❖ *Are you a classic problem solver? Find someone on your team whose clock runs much slower than yours. Use this person as a sounding board when urgent situations land on your desk.*

Avoid the "Love of Money" Trap

For the love of money is the root of all kinds of evil. And some people, craving money, have wandered from the true faith and pierced themselves with many sorrows.   *1 TIMOTHY 6:10*

When the big names go down in flames, they make CNN, but you don't need to be Enron, WorldCom, or Arthur Andersen to fall into the "love of money" trap. Plenty of small-fry executives find themselves "pierced with many sorrows" when their priorities get whacked.

Organizations run into trouble when

- decisions are based on profit margins rather than on what customers actually want;
- salaried employees are required to spend more time at work and less time with their families because of cutbacks;
- suppliers are squeezed for additional discounts beyond what is reasonable or necessary;
- executive-level staff are paid disproportionately more than the rank and file;
- wages are kept low because a glut of job seekers makes it easy to fill positions.

❖ *All resources come from God. Make financial decisions as if God were sitting next to you at the table, because he is.*

Look Back to Look Forward

God has sent me ahead of you to keep you and
your families alive. . . . So it was God who sent me
here, not you!   GENESIS 45:7-8

Joseph had finally revealed his identity to his
brothers, and they were justifiably afraid that he
would retaliate for their selling him into slavery.

Joseph, however, had a well-developed sense of historical perspective and knew that his current ability
to help them resulted from their actions taken many
years before.

If you want to know what will happen tomorrow,
pay attention to what occurred yesterday—especially
the events that looked bad at the time.

You may want to draw a quick map of the major
events in your organization's history, showing how
each significant step was built on something that
came before it.

❖ *Your ability to put current events into future
perspective will become more acute as you
learn to see how events of the past are woven
together by a common thread.*

Don't Think Like Everyone Else

The LORD has given me a strong warning not to think like everyone else does.   *ISAIAH 8:11*

Isaiah's assignment had nothing to do with getting the Israelites to sit around a campfire singing "Kumbaya." God hadn't asked him to be a team player. His job was to confront people with the reality of their situation and urge them to change.

In many ways, Isaiah was like a modern-day consultant who is hired to help an organization look at their circumstances from a different perspective. God was crystal clear on the approach that Isaiah should take:

Do not think like everyone else.

Doing so would waste time and perpetuate the problem. If people really wanted to change, they would have to listen to new ideas. Thinking the same thoughts was getting them nowhere.

When you go outside for new ideas, be careful not to feed the advisor too much of "this is how we do things around here."

❖ *Let the consultant observe and recommend from his or her unique perspective. Otherwise, you will waste your time and theirs.*

Bloom Where You're Planted

Work for the peace and prosperity of the city where I sent you into exile. Pray to the LORD for it, for its welfare will determine your welfare.
JEREMIAH 29:7

Corporate life can be a roller coaster. These days, entire divisions are handed from one company to another with the scratch of a pen on paper. One day you're working for ABC Widgets, and the next morning your parent company is XYZ Gizmos.

It can be hard to stay motivated, but that's what God wants you to do.

Jeremiah wrote a letter from God to the exiled Israelites. They would be in Babylon for seventy years, and he encouraged them to bloom where they were planted.

Everything you have is a gift from God. He is in charge, and if he plants you in a place you'd rather not be, your first responsibility is to do whatever you are asked to do in a manner that glorifies him.

❖ *Is it okay to ask God for a different assignment? You bet. But remember Jeremiah's words to the exiles: Plant gardens. Multiply. Do not dwindle away.*

Gouge Out Organizational Lust

So if your eye—even your good eye—causes you to lust, gouge it out and throw it away.   *MATTHEW 5:29*

Lust is an unhealthy desire for something you shouldn't have. It is most commonly regarded as a personal matter, but leaders also need to watch out for organizational lust.

The signs of a lustful organization are easy to spot:

Introduction of products that don't make sense to the core audiences

Reduction of quality or quantity with no reduction in prices

Decisions made with little or no diligent examination of the consequences

Expansion into new markets that place an unhealthy burden on resources

To avoid lustful activity, keep a steady eye on your mission. When attractive new ideas come along, challenge them by asking, "Will this take us toward our mission or away from it?"

Jesus warned that lustful desires could have a seed of good intention, but even if they come from your "good eye," you need to gouge them out if they don't support your organization's goals.

❖ *Has your organization been lusting after something it shouldn't have?*

Don't Worry About a Thing

So Potiphar gave Joseph complete administrative responsibility over everything he owned. With Joseph there, he didn't worry about a thing.
GENESIS 39:6

Take your pencil and circle the words *didn't worry* in the verse above. Potiphar obviously knew something about being an effective leader. After appointing Joseph as general manager of his household affairs, he no longer worried about them.

Potiphar wasn't looking over Joseph's shoulder or second-guessing his decisions.

As a leader, you need to let your people do what you hired them to do. One of the best ways to stay out of their hair is to concentrate on your own assignment, which is to look beyond the immediate landscape and plan for what you'll do in the future.

The Egyptian leader was fortunate to have a manager of Joseph's considerable ability, and he honored Joseph by not meddling in his affairs. If you share the same good fortune as Potiphar, be diligent in honoring your good managers by leaving them alone.

❖ Make it your goal to have someone say that you didn't worry about a thing.

Be Above Reproach

That Hebrew slave you've brought into our house tried to come in and fool around with me.
GENESIS 39:17

Potiphar could have paid more direct attention to his wife, but I'll leave that to the people who write marriage books.

Reality check: If you are in a position of authority, someone is going to tell lies about you.

You can't control the liars, so don't waste energy trying. You can, however, take steps to minimize the damage they cause.

Notice how Joseph was treated even when he was accused of a serious crime. He was sent to a prison where the king's prisoners were housed—a minimum-security, white-collar lockup.

Potiphar could have had Joseph killed, but he obviously had his doubts about the veracity of the claims against Joseph, probably because of Joseph's blameless record before the alleged incident.

❖ *As a leader, be above reproach in all that you do. Then, when the liars toss accusations your way, they won't have anything to stick to.*

Keep Being Who You Are

Before long, the warden put Joseph in charge of
. . . everything that happened in the prison. The
warden had no more worries, because Joseph took
care of everything. *GENESIS 39:22-23*

Job security isn't what it used to be. The typical
college graduate just entering the workforce will have
an estimated seven to ten different jobs over his or
her career. Some of the job changes will be voluntary,
but many will be the result of something outside
their control.

Unless you are in a unique situation, you will
probably be in transition at least once between now
and the time you stop working.

Involuntary job separation is tough. One way to
maintain your dignity is to keep doing what made
you successful in the first place. If you're an enthu-
siastic optimist, keep it up. If you're a bottom-line
realist, and it works for you, stay the course. Don't
let circumstances dictate who you are.

❖ *Joseph was tossed in jail for a crime he
didn't commit. Within a short time, he was back
doing what he had done all along.*

Network and Build Relationships

There was a young Hebrew man with us in the prison who was a slave of the captain of the guard. *GENESIS 41:12*

You probably know people with legendary Rolodex files. Ask them to suggest someone to help you distribute left-handed widget polishers in Panama City, and within minutes they're sending you an e-mail with a list of possibilities.

There seems to be too much emphasis these days on always needing to get something of value in return for a favor. I'm a classic networker, and more often than not, people think there are strings attached to my referrals. There aren't. All I ask is that you mention my name to the contact so they know where the referral came from. I know the favor will come back some day. It happens regularly.

Joseph worked for Potiphar, who introduced him to the prison warden, who connected him with the cupbearer, who mentioned his name to Pharaoh. What comes around goes around.

There is tremendous value in networking and building relationships.

❖ *How big is your Rolodex?*

Respect Everyone Equally

He gives his sunlight to both the evil and the good, and he sends rain on the just and the unjust alike.   *MATTHEW 5:45*

Dr. Bob Brower is the president of Point Loma Nazarene University, where our daughter is a student. When Bob walks through a crowded room, he clearly demonstrates that he has respect for everyone he meets.

Bob can't take more than five or six steps without someone tapping his arm and asking for a few minutes of his time. I've seen him chat with professors, parents, alumni donors, and students, all within a fifteen-minute walk through the dining commons. Each conversation is marked by Bob's singular attention to the person he's with. He shows equal regard for each person, regardless of who they are.

Jesus teaches that God doesn't play favorites. We all benefit from his love, regardless of our status.

Take a moment to consider how you treat people. Do you reserve special respect for those who might be more important?

❖ *I want to be more like Bob Brower. I hope you do too.*

Shake the Dust from Your Feet

If any household or town refuses to welcome you or listen to your message, shake its dust from your feet as you leave.   *MATTHEW 10:14*

In U.S. presidential politics, most states give their electoral college votes to the candidate receiving the most votes from state residents. Some states, however, are so heavily weighted to one side or the other that opposing candidates spend little time courting voters because this would be a waste of their resources.

Time, energy, and money are finite, and it's your job as the leader to waste as little of them as possible.

Marginal programs and products are the most obvious culprits, but the biggest drain is from people who refuse to listen.

Jesus told his disciples not to stay and keep preaching where they weren't welcome. There was only so much time, and he didn't want them to waste it.

❖ *What should you do about that handful of people who are constantly dragging your team down? What about potential customers who always have a reason for not buying? Take a lesson from the disciples and move on.*

Paint an Attractive Vision

After four generations your descendants will return here to this land.   GENESIS 15:16

If you're a leader, vision either comes naturally or after you've developed it over time. It may surprise you that most people aren't wired to look into the future and see much of anything on their own.

Human beings need someone to paint a picture of the future for them. They follow leaders—even those with questionable agendas—because the described future fills a void in the human need for vision.

God knew that Abram's offspring were in for a very long journey. He wanted to plant an attractive vision of the future in their hearts that would sustain them.

❖ *The appeal is not to a sense of duty, as in, "You are my chosen people, so you'd better suck it up and keep going." God's vision of the future is one of wonder and benefit. People respond better to a promise of reward than to a sense of duty.*

Don't Get in the Way

The people of Israel followed all of the LORD's instructions to Moses. Then Moses inspected all their work. When he found it had been done just as the LORD had commanded him, he blessed them. *EXODUS 39:42-43*

I was interviewing staff members for a client and heard more than one of them say something like, "We'd get a lot more done if we could get rid of the boss for a while."

It still makes me chuckle. The boss thought she was providing tremendous help when the opposite was actually true. She meant well, but she was too involved.

At the end of Exodus 39, Moses came to inspect the massive Tabernacle project.

Bezalel had been completely on his own. From the time Moses gave him the plans until the final garments were stitched, Moses was nowhere near the work.

Bezalel may have provided progress reports, but Moses let his foreman do what God had gifted him to do.

❖ *Perhaps you need to evaluate your involvement in some projects. Is there a chance you have been getting in the way?*

Don't Let the Past Stand in Your Way

David continued to succeed in everything he did, for the LORD was with him. When Saul recognized this, he became even more afraid of him.
1 SAMUEL 18:14-15

Here's a heads-up for young leaders: You pose a threat to those with more tenure because you represent change.

It's an unfortunate human characteristic, and I wish it were not true, but most people would rather fight than switch.

Don't rock the boat. . . . Try to fit in with the rest. . . . This is how we do it here.

Maintaining the status quo doesn't appear in anyone's corporate job description because doing so has become an established policy in far too many organizations.

David didn't back down. He was cautious and watched his back, but he also kept looking to the future. In 1 Samuel 18:16, we read that "all Israel and Judah loved David" because he was successful.

❖ *You have an imperative to lead; don't let the past stand in your way.*

Ask God for Success

O Lord, please hear my prayer! Listen to the prayers of those of us who delight in honoring you. Please grant me success today by making the king favorable to me. *NEHEMIAH 1:11*

Let's be crystal clear about something: Failure is *not* a fruit of the Spirit.

Why do so many leaders stop short of asking God for success? We pray that his will be done, but why do we assume that his will does not include granting us success in our endeavors?

Nehemiah had a plan that would restore the glory of Jerusalem and honor God. He presented his plan to the Lord and asked for success.

He didn't say, "I'll take whatever you give me."

Nehemiah stepped before God's throne and made his request: "Put it into [Artaxerxes'] heart to be kind to me" (Nehemiah 1:11).

Will your plans bring glory to God? Do you delight in honoring the Lord?

❖ *Have you asked him—specifically—for success?*

Seek Unity in Diversity

Yes, the body has many different parts, not just one part. If the foot says, "I am not a part of the body because I am not a hand," that does not make it any less a part of the body.   *1 CORINTHIANS 12:14-15*

My friend Glenn leads a large church choir that often performs with a full orchestra.

As he conducts 150 musician and singers, he has to focus on the big picture and the details at the same time.

As he leads, Glenn is able to hear the combined fullness of 150 voices and instruments blended as one.

At the same time, he is acutely aware of each person's performance; he is constantly adjusting individual pitch, volume, tempo, and tone quality in order to produce a uniform sound.

Paul points out the value of individual strengths. Each part should do what it does best, and it's the responsibility of the leader to help them all function as a single unit.

❖ *When you have the baton, make sure you're paying attention to the big picture and the details at the same time.*

Be a Helpful Mediator

A mediator is helpful if more than one party must reach an agreement.   *GALATIANS 3:20*

I'm often asked to arrange strategic partnerships for my clients in which two or more organizations combine efforts and resources to achieve related goals.

A retail store, a university admissions department, and a publisher might work together on a campaign that gives college students a free book if they register for class before a certain deadline.

The publisher gets titles in front of a target audience, the university gets the registration process finished sooner, and the retailer connects with potential customers.

The challenge is getting all three (or more) entities to agree on everything in a timely manner—and that's where the mediator comes in handy.

The mediator's job is to make the partnership work. He works for the alliance, not for the individual players, so his goal is to seek agreement from the individuals for the sake of the whole.

❖ *Blessed are those who make peace between disagreeing partners.*

Appreciate the Hierarchy

God said to Noah, "Yes, this rainbow is the sign of the covenant I am confirming with all the creatures on earth." *GENESIS 9:17*

I don't buy into the popular mantra that titles are unimportant in the workplace. The most common reason given for doing away with job titles is that they are just artificial badges of honor and that real leaders shouldn't need a title to show others who is in charge.

Go into any organization that claims to have eliminated titles and ask for the person in charge. There isn't a single person who doesn't know who the boss is or who reports to whom. There's a hierarchy, and everyone knows how it works.

Giving someone a title won't make them a better supervisor, but it will add a stratum of order that we humans seem to need. The title affirms that the organization believes this person can do the job they have been assigned.

❖ *God could simply have told Noah about his covenant to never again flood the earth, but he chose to mark the occasion with a sign.*

Prioritize Your Core Values

Then God gave the people all these
instructions. . . .   *EXODUS 20:1*

What is most important in your organization?

Is quality more important than innovation? Does
customer service take precedence over quality? Are
profits a higher priority than integrity?

Every organization needs a set of core values to
give employees a filter through which they can pass
critical decisions.

If customer service is more highly valued than
quality, an employee might decide to release a
product that is slightly imperfect in order to fill a
customer's need on time. Of course, integrity should
be the highest value, so in this example, the employee
would be up-front with the customer about the quality issue.

It's not enough to have a list of core values. They
need to be prioritized so there's no question about
which has a higher value when push comes to shove.

❖ *Have you given your team a list of "com-
mandments" to help them make decisions when
you're not there to make the call?*

Speak the Truth in Love

We will speak the truth in love. *EPHESIANS 4:15*

Christian kids are taught to lie at church potlucks.

Every church has one or two women whose taste buds have been burned off by too much hot coffee. Do their families actually eat this stuff? Do they try out new recipes at potlucks?

The worst I ever experienced were yummy-looking meatballs—made from liver.

No kidding.

Of course, you're never allowed to speak the truth: "Mommy, this smells like poop."

Seriously, we have a tendency to sit quietly while someone does something poorly or wrong or inappropriate, because we think that loving someone requires us to remain silent.

Paul presents an argument to the contrary. Not speaking up is actually a disservice.

The balance for leaders is not easy. You want to be patient, kind, and tolerant of error, but you have a mission to accomplish, and lousy work, mistakes, and poor judgment hinder everyone's efforts.

The critical words are *in love*.

❖ *If you really love someone, you tell them the truth.*

When It's Time to Move, Move!

When Abram heard that his nephew Lot had been captured, he mobilized the 318 trained men who had been born into his household. *GENESIS 14:14*

It was the deciding game of the World Series. My team's comfortable lead dwindled away until the opposition was just one run away from tying the game and two runs away from taking the championship.

Much of the lead had been siphoned off in the last two innings due to serious errors by a legendary pitcher who wasn't performing up to par.

No one could figure out why the manager hadn't brought in a reliever. When another batter connected and drove home the tying run, you could see the fire go out of my team. A new pitcher was brought in, but it was too late.

Abram knew he was the only one who could rescue Lot, and he didn't hesitate to do what needed to be done. Hesitation would have sealed Lot's doom.

❖ *There is a time for waiting and a time for action. When it's time to move, move!*

Be a Blessing to Others

I will make you into a great nation. I will bless you and make you famous, and you will be a blessing to others. *GENESIS 12:2*

The idea of being famous trips up a lot of leaders—on either side of the equation.

Some, caught up in the excitement of celebrity, lose sight of who they really are. Others avoid any situation that might place them in the spotlight, and thus miss the opportunity to do what God created them to do.

If you're part of the first group, enjoy the ride, because I've never seen it last as long as you'd like it to.

If you're part of the second group, remember that leadership always brings some level of honor.

People can't follow what they can't see.

Even if you're leading a very small organization, you'll be famous to your staff. It's just a matter of degree.

❖ *The secret to keeping your head on straight is in the last half of the verse. Read it over and over, and you'll do just fine.*

Count the Cost

Don't begin until you count the cost. *LUKE 14:28*

Let me turn the tables and first share what I believe this passage is *not* saying. I don't believe Jesus is encouraging his followers to move forward only if they are certain of the future. That would be inconsistent with his message of faith.

On the contrary, I think Jesus is telling us to consider the cost of anything we undertake so we can begin with complete understanding of the price we will pay.

It is in the nature of leadership to move into unknown territory. Doing so requires a certain amount of faith, because no one can accurately predict the future.

Effective leaders are willing to take reasonable risks based on informed decisions after weighing potential benefits against their best estimates of what it will take to succeed.

Don't move too fast, and don't wait too long.

❖ *When the time is right, pour on the steam, and know that you've made the best decision.*

Recognize Wise Counsel

Whenever the king consulted them in any matter requiring wisdom and balanced judgment, he found them ten times more capable than any of the magicians and enchanters in his entire kingdom.

DANIEL 1:20

Hats off to Nebuchadnezzar! Surrounded by a host of smooth-talking con men, he turned to Daniel and his countrymen for genuine solutions to important questions.

When Nebuchadnezzar didn't seek Daniel's advice, the results were tragic. The king actually went insane for a period of time and ate grass like a cow (try to cover *that* gap in your résumé during a job interview).

The ability to recognize wise counsel is an important leadership quality.

It is one that develops over time, through trial and unfortunate error. Having a handful of trusted advisors is worth more than you could ever pay them, so cherish and protect these relationships as the treasures they are.

❖ *Take a moment to run an inventory of your trusted advisors. To whom do you turn when faced with a matter requiring wisdom and balanced judgment?*

Accept Applause Graciously

It is not because I am wiser than anyone else that I know the secret of your dream, but because God wants you to understand what was in your heart.   *DANIEL 2:30*

The congressman was bragging about an important piece of legislation he had cosponsored. When reporters pressed him for details, he was evasive because he had never actually seen the bill. His name had been attached to the measure so he could brag to the folks back home about cosponsoring it.

Even though Daniel was wiser than most of the people surrounding Nebuchadnezzar, he set the record straight by revealing the source of his wisdom. The king's respect for Daniel and his God deepened.

If you live by a creed of giving credit where it's due, you are also required to accept credit when you deserve it. There is no reason for false modesty. If you do something praiseworthy, accept the applause graciously.

❖ *Take time to publicly acknowledge those on your team who have contributed to a success—they'll appreciate the applause as well.*

Enhance Your Reputation

A good reputation is more valuable than costly perfume.   *ECCLESIASTES 7:1*

Here's a quick anatomy lesson: The area of your brain that controls the sense of smell is right next to the area that controls your emotions. That's why certain aromas, such as perfumes or Grandma's oatmeal cookies, produce such strong emotional responses.

The author of Ecclesiastes understood the emotional power of a reputation.

Costly perfume elicits a strong emotional response, but he says that this is nothing compared to the emotional strength of your reputation.

How do you smell?

Your image influences people's attitude toward you more than anything you say or do. Your reputation is the aroma that precedes you. It colors the response people will have to your leadership, even before they meet you.

People follow leaders with whom they have a strong emotional connection. Your reputation—your image—is the glue that holds that connection together.

Do you pay attention to how you are perceived?

❖ *Your reputation precedes you. What does it say before you arrive?*

Lend a Hand

Abraham was 100 years old when Isaac was born. And Sarah declared, "God has brought me laughter." *GENESIS 21:5-6*

Sarah wanted nothing more than to give her husband a son, despite the fact that they were both very old. When God granted her the desire of her heart, she was overcome with joy to the point that she exploded in laughter.

The laughter was contagious. It became an epidemic. I can imagine that everyone who knew Sarah started laughing for joy when they heard the news. People knew that God had given Sarah what she had longed for all those years.

How often do you bring joyful laughter to the lives of the people you lead?

As a leader, you can help your people achieve their goals. The first step is to know what's important in their lives and then to ask them if there is any way you can help. God didn't just hand Sarah a baby. She did the work, but she acknowledged the role Yahweh played in her success.

❖ *Your people aren't looking for a handout, just a hand up.*

Let Outsiders Spread the Word

Some wise men from eastern lands arrived in Jerusalem, asking, "Where is the newborn king of the Jews . . . ?" King Herod was deeply disturbed when he heard this.   *MATTHEW 2:1-3*

My client's potential customers thought they were familiar with his product, but it was clear from their comments that they didn't know much about it.

When people think they have all the facts, they turn a deaf ear to anything new you have to say.

This is called the Paradox of Familiarity.

To reach around this dilemma, find individuals who are not familiar with your story, get them excited about it, and let them deliver the new information to your audience.

King Herod and the Jewish leaders thought they had God all figured out. They weren't open to new information and didn't even notice the commotion in Bethlehem. God used outsiders to give the religious leaders a wake-up call.

❖ *If you're having trouble getting through to people who think they have it all figured out, perhaps you should start telling your story to someone else.*

Explain Your Mission

When the Pharisees saw this, they asked his disciples, "Why does your teacher eat with such scum?" When Jesus heard this, he said, "Healthy people don't need a doctor—sick people do."
MATTHEW 9:11-12

There's a delicate balance between turning the other cheek and defending your mission against malicious attacks.

If the naysayer attacks you personally by questioning your integrity or maligning your beliefs, it is probably best to ignore them. They don't respect you, and it's unlikely that they'll listen to your defense.

If their comments are directed against the mission and what you are trying to accomplish, it's your responsibility to make a strong defense.

When the Pharisees attacked Jesus' character, he turned it around. Instead of saying, "You have it wrong about me," he said, "You are mistaken about what I am trying to do."

Perhaps you are criticized as an irresponsible risk taker, or as being too eager for change. Instead of defending yourself, help your critics to understand what you are trying to accomplish.

❖ *Jesus regarded his mission as more important than his personal reputation. You should too.*

State Your Intentions Up Front

Then food was served. But Abraham's servant said, "I don't want to eat until I have told you why I have come." *GENESIS 24:33*

It is said that baseball legend Babe Ruth would taunt opposing pitchers by pointing to the outfield as if to say, "I'm going to hit a home run over that spot in the wall."

I'm not sure how many times he actually did that, or how often he was able to deliver on his threat, but I admire his stating his intentions right up front.

Abraham's servant wanted Laban to know exactly what his objective was before they had dinner. He was there to find a wife for Isaac. Once Laban and the servant were on the same page, the negotiations could begin.

❖ *You won't lose any advantage by stating your objectives right up front. Laying your cards on the table at the onset will give both sides a clear picture of the objective you are trying to achieve, which makes the process much easier.*

Discipline Staff Fairly

The punishment must match the injury: a life for a life, an eye for an eye, a tooth for a tooth, a hand for a hand, a foot for a foot, a burn for a burn, a wound for a wound, a bruise for a bruise.   *EXODUS 21:23-25*

Overheard in the lunchroom:

"Wow, Jane messed up, but I think Nancy went a bit overboard by suspending her."

"Yeah, it makes me wonder what they care about more—us or their precious profits."

People have an intrinsic sense of justice, and they know whether or not the punishment is appropriate.

Going overboard with punishments can cause long-lasting damage, and people may doubt your motives. It's nearly impossible to lead people who are questioning your integrity.

Folks trust you to make the right decision in every situation. They will be lenient if you're fair, but you'll lose them if they sense that you've stepped over the line.

When you have the unfortunate task of punishing someone, take great pains to be fair.

❖ *Justice may be blind, but it requires tremendous balance.*

Publicize Delegated Authority

Stay here and wait for us until we come back.
Aaron and Hur are here with you. If anyone has
a dispute while I am gone, consult with them.

EXODUS 24:14

Moses put Aaron and Hur in charge while he was
gone. He also made the critically important step
of announcing this to the regional managers. It's
not enough to give someone the responsibility of
"running the place while I'm gone." There needs to
be clear communication to the entire organization
that the baton has been passed.

Leaving someone in charge without making a
public acknowledgment is like sending someone out
to police the streets in regular clothes, with no badge,
in an unmarked car.

People shouldn't simply have authority bestowed
on them. They should earn it, but your absence
creates a void that must be filled by someone who is
clearly in charge.

Announcing someone to represent your authority
doesn't give them anything except an opportunity to
prove themselves worthy of the appointment.

❖ *Your people should never have to say, "Hey,
who's in charge here, anyway?"*

Practice Creative Solutions

All the bridesmaids got up and prepared their lamps. Then the five foolish ones asked the others, "Please give us some of your oil because our lamps are going out." *MATTHEW 25:7-8*

This parable can motivate you to examine your organization's ability to think creatively about Plan B solutions.

Ten young women were invited to a wedding. Five of them brought extra oil to keep their lamps burning in the event the bridegroom was delayed (and I thought that only happened in the movies).

The other five (Jesus calls them "foolish") didn't bring extra oil, and when the groom was delayed, their lamps went out.

Read the entire passage (Matthew 25:1-13) to your team and ask, How could the five foolish bridesmaids have handled this differently?

Look beyond the simple answer, which is that they should have brought enough oil.

There are other possible solutions. Asking your leadership team to brainstorm possible scenarios will get them thinking about Plan B ideas for your unique situation.

❖ *Practice your ability to find creative solutions. Have fun with this one.*

Be Real

All of Judea . . . went out to see and hear John.
. . . His clothes were woven from coarse camel hair,
and he wore a leather belt around his waist. For
food he ate locusts and wild honey.   MARK 1:5-6

There's a Trader Joe's receipt sitting near my chair.
Trader Joe's is a chain of specialty food stores with a
unique image.

The store's circular appears to be pasted together
by someone with very little graphic-design training.
There are no color photos of big juicy hams to catch
my eye.

The stores are similarly unmodern. No conveyor
belts carry purchased items. Most checkers wear jeans
and T-shirts (some are tie-dyed).

And the place is always packed with people. *Normal* people.

John the Baptist was a pretty weird guy for first-
century Palestine, yet people were drawn to him,
even the normal people who lived in Jerusalem.

Both are lessons in the power of authenticity.
People were drawn to John, as they are to Trader
Joe's, because they could sense his genuineness.

❖ *How real are you, really?*

Use the Hierarchy

Call for your brother, Aaron, and his sons. . . . Set them apart from the rest of the people of Israel so they may . . . be my priests.   *EXODUS 28:1*

I wish I had a dollar for every time I've seen one of those graphs depicting a flat organizational structure.

Someone is always coming up with another idea for taking the hierarchy out of corporate structures.

Talk to the leaders in these companies (you'll find them in the larger offices) and quiz them about why they went flat. They will respond with words such as *shifting the lines of authority, decentralizing the authority model,* or similar mumbo jumbo.

The bottom line is that these ideas are neither effective nor based on biblical truth.

Aaron and his sons were set apart from the rest.

❖ *We are created equal in God's sight, and each person is worthy, but someone is always set apart to lead. Someone always decides which holidays are going to be paid and when folks can wear jeans to the office.*

Make Promotions Special

This is the ceremony you must follow when you consecrate Aaron and his sons to serve me as priests. *EXODUS 29:1*

Think about the first time you were promoted to a position that really meant something. It wasn't a popularity contest; it meant that you had certain abilities and were valued by the organization.

Such events are special milestones in a person's life. The next time you are able to offer someone a significant promotion, pay careful attention to how you tell him or her about your decision.

Think about taking this person to lunch or dinner. Try crafting a great letter that explains why you feel he or she is the right person for the job. If you have time, order business cards with the person's new title, and hand them over when you offer him or her the job.

Whatever you do, don't rush through the process. Let them savor the moment. Give them time to ask questions.

❖ *Show them that this is the best decision you've made in a long time.*

Maintain a Consistent Identity

Jesus said, "No, go home to your family, and tell them everything the Lord has done for you and how merciful he has been." So the man . . . began to proclaim the great things Jesus had done for him.   *MARK 5:19-20*

The strength of any organization is found in its ability to be in multiple locations.

Make this work by ensuring that everyone is reading from the same playbook. Expanding your influence can quickly become a liability if your message isn't consistent from one place to another.

Jesus gave specific instructions to the man he healed without putting words in his mouth. He did not attempt to mislead him or spin the story. Jesus gave the man directions that would maintain the consistency of the message in a new place.

As you expand into new markets or send people to remote locations, take time to develop communication guidelines so that everyone on the team knows what to say and how to say it.

❖ *E pluribus unum—one out of many.*

Take Research Results to Heart

Let their bountiful table become a snare, a trap that makes them think all is well.   *ROMANS 11:9*

If you're planning to conduct some market research, heed Paul's warning and avoid the arrogance of success.

I've watched healthy organizations sponsor comprehensive market studies only to ignore findings that didn't support predetermined assumptions. Since they were doing well, they argued with results that indicated a need for change in the status quo.

The purpose of conducting research is to find out what you don't know.

If findings support your current plans, you have cause to celebrate. If they don't, celebrate even more, because a light has been turned on in the darkness.

Paul quotes from Psalm 69 when describing people who have all the evidence they need to make an informed decision but refuse to accept the facts. He describes them as being in a deep sleep, with their eyes shut and their ears closed.

❖ *If you're wise enough to sponsor research, wake up and pay attention to what it tells you.*

Protect Yourself with Contracts

Write down all these instructions, for they represent the terms of the covenant I am making with you and with Israel. *EXODUS 34:27*

Written contracts are like Listerine mouthwash, which once had the advertising slogan,

"The taste you hate to use, twice a day."

The stuff tastes awful, but it works.

Inherent in every contract is the implication that someone might not keep their commitment. Most contracts have language that spells out—before the work even starts—what will happen if the work isn't completed or payment isn't made.

There is also something liberating about a contract. Contracts present formal recognition that two parties have come to an agreement. A signed document indicates that both sides intend to work within certain parameters to accomplish something.

Don't be afraid to suggest a contract when one is appropriate.

If your word and your handshake are good enough, then a signed contract is even better. It's a promise taken to the next level.

❖ *God insisted on a written covenant. You should too.*

Take a Positive Stand

Caleb tried to quiet the people as they stood before Moses. "Let's go at once to take the land," he said. "We can certainly conquer it!"
NUMBERS 13:30

Caleb is my hero. I use his story to boost my spirits when people think I'm "too far out" and my ideas are impossible.

Moses sent Caleb and eleven other men to scout out Canaan, saying, "Tell me what we have to look forward to and what we'll be up against."

The place was awesome, with milk, honey, and incredible fruit, but ten of the scouts said, "There is no way we can do this. We should be satisfied with what we have."

Caleb disagreed. "I'm not saying that it will be easy, but look at this fruit! Come on—we can do this!"

If you're a Caleb, take heart. God has a special place for you. Caleb was honored for the stand he took.

❖ *If you have a Caleb on your team, keep him (or her) healthy. It was Caleb who helped the Israelites move forward.*

Excite People's Emotions

All whose hearts were stirred and whose spirits were moved came and brought their sacred offerings to the LORD.   *EXODUS 35:21*

Three elements are inherent in any effective marketing campaign. I call them the "Three *E*s":

Engage their attention,

Excite their emotions, and

Energize them to act.

This verse is a great example of the second *E, Excite* their emotions.

It wasn't obligation that motivated the people to make sacrificial gifts. They were moved by a vision.

Read further and find the word *willingly* (Exodus 35:23). They weren't forced, coerced, or shamed into participating. Logic and responsibility aren't mentioned.

They were given a glimpse of the future in Moses' vivid description of God's plans for the Tabernacle, and they wanted to be part of it.

❖ *One aspect of great leadership is the ability to excite people's emotions.*

Transcend Sibling Rivalry

They scoffed, "He's just a carpenter, the son of Mary and the brother of James, Joseph, Judas, and Simon. And his sisters live right here among us." They were deeply offended and refused to believe in him. *MARK 6:3*

My friend Alice Davis is a psychologist who studies what happens to relationships among coworkers when one of them is promoted to management. She describes the resulting ill will as a form of sibling rivalry.

We have trouble accepting that someone who "grew up" with us can be different from what they have always been, which is "one of us."

Jesus faced this same dilemma, and Mark writes that Jesus "was amazed at their unbelief" (Mark 6:6).

It's clear from Mark's report that Jesus didn't waste time trying to convince them otherwise. There's no evidence that he went out of his way to win them over.

Jesus didn't allow these folks to get in the way of his mission. He recognized the situation, dealt with it, and moved on.

❖ *Has sibling rivalry clouded your mission focus? Decide today that you'll accept it as unavoidable human nature and move on.*

Shine Some Light

Your eye is a lamp that provides light for your body. When your eye is good, your whole body is filled with light. *LUKE 11:34*

When you drive fast on a busy highway, your eyes constantly gather data that helps you make critical decisions about how to reach your destination safely. Taking your eyes off the road for even a few seconds can be disastrous. You can't rely on the view you had ten seconds ago because everything around you has changed.

Jesus uses the eye as a metaphor for any source of illumination that shines truth into darkness. He warns against trusting a bad eye that fills a room with darkness.

One responsibility of a leader is to make sure the organization has an adequate source of light. As in the driving example, it's critical that decisions be based on current, truthful information. Decisions made in the dark usually result in fatal errors.

❖ *Think about the decisions you will make in the next twenty-four hours. Are you confident that your eyes have been gathering truthful illumination? Does your organization have a steady stream of good light?*

Stay on Track

Be careful to obey all the instructions Moses gave
you. . . . Meditate on [them] day and night.
JOSHUA 1:7-8

Wordspy.com, an online dictionary of newly coined
phrases, defines *mission creep* as follows: "mission
creep *noun*. The process by which an [organization's]
goals change gradually over time."

You've probably heard someone say, "I don't know
where we got off track, but we're heading in the
wrong direction."

It happens so subtly that it is barely noticeable,
and because it happens over time, the "new mission"
is difficult to reverse.

Leaders are often tempted to shift priorities when
solving immediate problems. Relaxing your commitment to core values for a quick fix can lead to mission creep.

God told Joshua to maintain his focus by consistently meditating on it. The goal was burned into his
heart, and he never took his eyes off the prize.

❖ *Every leader faces mission creep. Can you
identify areas in which your current activity
is not directed toward the primary objective?
Be on guard against the lure of short-term
solutions.*

Don't Rely on Past Success

Joshua secretly sent out two spies from the Israelite camp. . . . "Scout out the land on the other side
of the Jordan River." *JOSHUA 2:1*

If you've been in a successful leadership position
for a significant amount of time, you are highly
susceptible to a malady I refer to as "The Paradox of
Experience."

This is especially true of those who have led the
same organization or have been in the same industry
for a while. Experience can be a great teacher; it can
also lull you into poor decisions based on yesterday's
knowledge.

It's impossible to accurately predict the future,
but the likelihood of your coming close to the mark
improves in relation to the freshness of your knowledge.

Joshua was a successful leader with Yahweh on
his side. The Israelites were within striking distance
of the Promised Land. They had focused on this for
hundreds of years, but he still took time to update
his knowledge.

❖ *As a leader, it is tempting to rely on past success. Don't let experience lead you astray.*

Make Contingency Plans

A servant who knows what the master wants, but isn't prepared and doesn't carry out those instructions, will be severely punished. But someone who does not know, and then does something wrong, will be punished only lightly.   *LUKE 12:47-48*

Part of our charm as human beings is our innate ability to mess things up. We lie, cheat, steal, make mistakes, and forget things.

People will let us down—that's a constant. The variable is how we deal with it. In this passage, Jesus provides some advice on human frailty.

Set aside time to preplan your responses to various manifestations of people's humanity. Think through what you will do when someone steals from or cheats you. Consider how you will handle a trusted employee who forgets to complete a critical task.

I'm not suggesting that you *plan* to be let down. Instead, focus on how you might respond to various situations.

❖ *You have contingency plans for mechanical breakdowns. It makes sense to have a Plan B that covers inevitable disappointments from the human beings on your team.*

Avoid Ambiguity

As surely as God is faithful, my word to you does not waver between "Yes" and "No." For Jesus Christ, the Son of God, does not waver between "Yes" and "No." *2 CORINTHIANS 1:18-19*

It's nearly impossible to hear a politician talk about issues these days without sensing ulterior motives. No matter what they say, you wonder what they really mean because their answers are so couched in political jargon.

Paul follows Jesus' example by not getting caught in the gray area between "Yes" and "No." As far as Paul is concerned, there's no wiggle room when it comes to the truth.

If your desire as a leader is to earn and maintain the respect of those who follow you, it's vitally important that you clearly define your opinions and objectives.

If you feel strongly about something, state your case. If you're ambivalent, be very clear about the points you're struggling with.

❖ *If you play with all your cards facing out, no one will accuse you of compromising your integrity for the sake of convenience.*

Slow Down and Prepare

When this happened, I did not rush out to consult with any human being. Nor did I go up to Jerusalem. . . . Instead, I went away into Arabia, and later I returned to the city of Damascus. Then three years later I went to Jerusalem.   *GALATIANS 1:16-18*

A common assumption is that Paul began his ministry immediately after his Damascus Road experience. In fact, he spent three years in seclusion, getting ready for what lay ahead.

He didn't rush.

He knew how important the job was and took time to prepare.

Most projects that are rushed to market either fail or need to be fixed soon after they get off the ground. The more time you take to plan a project, the greater the likelihood it will be successful.

I'm not suggesting that protracted planning cycles will save a bad idea, nor am I advocating multiple unnecessary reviews, but taking appropriate care in planning and preparing is a practice we don't see enough of these days.

❖ *Slow down; life is too important to rush.*

Be a Lifelong Learner

The LORD told Joshua, "Today I will begin to make you a great leader in the eyes of all the Israelites." *JOSHUA 3:7*

Moses had died, and God was preparing to take the Israelites over the Jordan River into the Promised Land.

Joshua had been Moses' assistant since childhood. The people knew his name, and stories about his abilities had spread throughout the tribes. He was the man of the hour.

As Israel stood at the edge of the river waiting for instructions, God said that he would now begin to make Joshua a great leader in the eyes of the people.

There is more than one lesson in this:

God sometimes puts us in positions before we're completely ready, so we have to trust him.

Celebrity only makes you famous; it doesn't necessarily make you a leader.

Your ability to lead depends on the team's perception of you, not on your résumé.

❖ *Joshua was at the beginning of a leadership development course that never ended. At what stage of the learning process are you?*

Don't Stand on Your Rights

Thank God for your good sense! Bless you for keeping me from murder and from carrying out vengeance with my own hands.   *1 SAMUEL 25:33*

David had been wronged by a grouchy old man named Nabal, and he had the right to seek vengeance by killing him (things were different back then).

Nabal's wife, Abigail, convinced David to change his mind by presenting a reasonable argument for allowing God to deal with her husband.

Abigail helped David see that standing up for his rights would leave Nabal's blood on his hands forever.

David caught a glimpse of the potentially devastating results of his plan, and he didn't like what he saw. He was thankful for the opportunity to change direction.

There are times when demanding your rights can cause more harm than good.

❖ *How often have you been burdened with the consequences of standing on principle?*

Honor Everyone Equally

His father said to him, "Look, dear son, you have always stayed by me, and everything I have is yours. We had to celebrate this happy day. For your brother . . . has come back to life!"   *LUKE 15:31-32*

In most organizations, a couple of departments are usually at odds with each other over something.

Sales is angry with Accounting because of credit holds placed on big customers.

Production has issues with Marketing because the new package design was turned in after the deadline. Everyone thinks IT should be more proactive, and IT thinks people should learn how to reboot their own PCs.

In the midst of this, a handful of great leaders navigate the twists and turns of departmental rivalries with the skill of Olympic downhill skiers. They honor everyone equally.

The main focus of the Prodigal Son story is the grace shown to the home-coming boy. Jesus also gives us a glimpse into the father's leadership skill with the brief exchange between the older son and his dad.

❖ *The father didn't play favorites. Do you?*

Do Something Unusual

The woman was surprised.   *JOHN 4:9*

I am a huge fan of improvisational comedy. When a really good improv comic is on stage, I am glued to the edge of my seat. Experience tells me that it's going to be surprising and funny, so I pay strict attention to every word.

Being unpredictable is one of the best ways to get someone's attention. If you repeat the same message too many times, people will ignore you. If they think they already know what you're going to say, they will stop paying attention.

Jesus was a master of unpredictability.

The woman at the well was shocked that Jesus would speak to her, let alone ask her for a drink of water. He also surprised her by telling her things she thought no one else knew. In so doing, Jesus captured her attention, and quite possibly her heart.

❖ *Take time to understand how others perceive your organization. Are you so predictable that folks have begun to ignore your messages? Without changing what you stand for, could you get their attention by doing something unusual?*

Give Honest Encouragement

We are pressed on every side by troubles, but we are not crushed. We are perplexed, but not driven to despair. We are hunted down, but never abandoned by God. We get knocked down, but we are not destroyed.   *2 CORINTHIANS 4:8-9*

Have you ever been to a sporting event where the home team played "We Are the Champions" by Queen?

> We are the champions, my friend,
> And we'll keep on fighting 'til the end.
> We are the champions.
> We are the champions.
> No time for losers, 'cause we are
> The champions of the world.

The song works great when the team is winning, but it sounds ridiculous when fortunes are reversed.

Paul the apostle was no stranger to hardship. He encouraged the church to rely on God, but he didn't paste on a phony smile. While facing situations realistically, Paul reminded them that "great power is from God" (2 Corinthians 4:7).

Perhaps your team is going through difficult times.

Your best path is to give honest encouragement. They don't need a cheerleader, but a leader who understands their dilemmas and offers a credible solution.

❖ *Put away the pom-poms and be real.*

Groom a Number Two

God said to Noah, "I have decided . . ."
GENESIS 6:13

I have enjoyed observing a handful of people that I refer to as "Number Two" individuals. A Number Two stands in the shadow of a person in the spotlight and makes them look good.

It's not an easy job, but when done properly, it is beautiful to watch. There is a good example of this in the movie *The American President,* starring Michael Douglas as the president and Martin Sheen as his longtime chief of staff.

In the movie, the two men are best friends. They have worked together since college, yet out of respect for his office, Sheen's character never calls his friend by his first name.

As the Number Two, Sheen's character understands his mission completely and knows that he is playing a vital role. As human beings, they are equals, but in practicality, one of them is the president.

❖ *When God needed someone he could trust to carry out a special mission, he found a strong Number Two in Noah. Who can you groom to be your Number Two?*

Explain Your Reasons

Look! I am about to cover the earth with a flood that will destroy every living thing that breathes.   *GENESIS 6:17*

A trait that sets humans apart from animals is their need to ask why. We have an intrinsic need to have things explained to us.

Britt Beemer, a nationally renowned consumer-research specialist, says shoppers will react more positively to a sale if there is a reason for it. Beemer's research has shown that you'll get better results from a "Spring Sale" than you will from a "(no name) sale" that happens to run at the same time.

People have a subconscious need to know *why* you are running a sale. God understood this and made sure that Noah knew why he was building the ark.

❖ *Perhaps you are trying to get your staff, customers, or organization to move on a certain project. Take the time to explain why you're asking them to do this. It's especially necessary when you are asking them to do something they have never done before—such as build an ark.*

Facilitate Staff Compliance

Noah did everything exactly as God had commanded him.   GENESIS 6:22

Read that verse over about five times. Now, please resist the urge to run an ad that says,

"Wanted: One or two Noahs to make my life easier."

Here are some secrets to having your staff do everything exactly as you command:

Let them know you trust them. God encouraged
    Noah by making a covenant with him.
Give them the big picture. People need to know
    where they fit into your overall plans.
Let them know you're in charge. I'm sure Noah
    had complete trust in God's ability to do what
    he said he would do.
Get out of the way and let them do what you've
    hired them to do.

God must have kept an eye on Noah as he built the ark, but he didn't cut the lumber or spread tar in the cracks.

❖ *God drew up the plans, shared his vision, and offered encouragement. And Noah did "everything exactly as God had commanded him."*

Empower with Information

Seven days from now I will make the rains pour down on the earth.   *GENESIS 7:4*

God was getting ready to carry out his plan to wipe the earth clean of evil, which was something he had never done before.

His man on the job was making final preparations for the world-changing event, and God took time to explain the details of his plan to Noah.

It isn't mentioned, but we can assume the ark generated some curiosity in the region. As his point person on the project, God knew that Noah would be answering some interesting questions from the locals, so he gave Noah a step-by-step timeline for what was going to happen.

❖ *If you are embarking on a controversial new activity, make sure the people on the front lines know what is going to happen. If you have a spokesperson, give them everything they need to do their job, because providing half an answer is worse than no answer, and no answer is pretty bad.*

Conduct Adequate Research

He also released a dove to see if the water had
receded and it could find dry ground. *GENESIS 8:8*

Nothing is more disastrous than someone in a
leadership position who thinks he knows market
realities and refuses to conduct adequate research.

This is called "the arrogance of success."

It results from someone relying on past experience
to make decisions that will affect the future. What
worked in the past will not necessarily work in the
future because the future will be different.

Urgency is no excuse for moving ahead without
solid data to back you up. Noah had been on the ark
for a very long time, but he took the time to update
his knowledge about the surrounding environment.
Any decision he made would affect the future of the
entire human race, so he wanted to get it right.

❖ *I can't sufficiently stress the importance of
good research. Having data to back up your
decisions will give you an added level of confidence and reduce the need to go back and fix
things once they're out of the barn—or the ark.*

Anticipate People's Needs

Then Jesus called his disciples and told them, "I feel sorry for these people. They have been here with me for three days, and they have nothing left to eat. I don't want to send them away hungry, or they will faint along the way." *MATTHEW 15:32*

As a good leader, Jesus was aware of people's needs. His amazing connection with people and his ability to anticipate their needs came from a genuine understanding of their condition. He must have drawn on his personal experience of being hungry in the wilderness in order to relate to what they were feeling.

As a leader, it's tempting to focus on the future and forget about the past, leaving followers to fend for themselves as they scramble to keep up.

Jesus stopped and looked back to make sure his followers were able to keep up. Do you remember what it was like to be part of the crowd?

❖ *If your followers can't follow, you're no longer leading.*

Plant Generously

Remember this—a farmer who plants only a few seeds will get a small crop. But the one who plants generously will get a generous crop.
2 CORINTHIANS 9:6

The CFO of a medium-size church had trouble with the proposed budget, which exceeded giving from the previous year. The staff saw potential for growth, but the CFO argued intensely for a budget reduction. He thought their plans were foolish.

During a heated discussion, the CFO demanded a guarantee that the new funding level would be achieved. The pastor's response was brilliant: "I can't guarantee we'll meet this goal. But I guarantee we'll never meet it if we don't try. If we want a larger crop, we have to plant more seeds."

The early church was growing, and Paul encouraged the believers to invest in the future.

Wanting to grow is good stewardship, and good stewardship requires investment—in people, facilities, marketing, strategic planning, and core competencies. A few organizations grow despite themselves, but these are the exceptions, not the rule.

❖ *You can't harvest what you don't plant.*

Review People's Work

After a long time their master returned from his trip and called them to give an account of how they had used his money.   *MATTHEW 25:19*

A friend of mine shared some frustrations recently—her boss requires people to submit lengthy and detailed reports of their activities, but apparently never actually reads them.

"He checks his e-mail to make sure we've submitted them on time," she said, "but he asks questions I've already answered in the report."

In this parable, Jesus tells of three servants who were each entrusted by their master with an amount of silver. On his return, each servant presented the results of their investment and received an appropriate reward for their efforts.

The story is about being a good servant, but there's also a lesson in it for leaders:

People feel devalued if an assignment isn't inspected, especially if they've put in extra effort to do a really great job.

❖ *Honor your people by reviewing their work and rewarding them for a job well done.*

Revisit Changed Situations

We can plainly see that the LORD is with you. So we want to enter into a sworn treaty with you. Let's make a covenant. *GENESIS 26:28*

One of the advantages of being in leadership is the opportunity to take your eyes off the nitty-gritty and concentrate on the big picture. You hire managers to tend the flock while you walk through the hills looking for new pastures.

Sometimes those new pastures will be places you've already visited that weren't ready for your flock the first time around. Customers who left can return. Competitors can become allies. A supplier who raised prices beyond your comfort zone can make a new offer.

Isaac and Abimelech were bitter enemies at one time, but now in a different environment, they took an oath of cooperation. Isaac was wary at first because Abimelech had treated him harshly a few years before, but Abimelech saw some advantages in a treaty with Isaac, and Isaac agreed.

❖ *It's okay to revisit situations that have changed through time and circumstance.*

Prepare Talking Points

Jacob gave the same instructions to the second and third herdsmen and to all who followed behind the herds: "You must say the same thing to Esau when you meet him." GENESIS 32:19

If your organization has more than one person who might be asked for comments on a particular project, prepare formal lists of talking points so everyone will know what they are supposed to say.

This is not an attempt to gloss over the truth or stifle individualism; it is a valuable lesson that you, as a leader, would not want to learn the hard way.

This practice isn't only used by spin doctors and professional liars. Your image is your most valuable asset, and preparing a short list of points on key issues will help you to avoid having to explain which one of two or three answers to the same question is actually the truth.

❖ *When reporters, customers, employees, or anyone else asks a question, you must all say the same thing.*

Look beyond Appearances

When Jesus came by, he looked up at Zacchaeus and called him by name. "Zacchaeus!" he said. "Quick, come down! I must be a guest in your home today." *LUKE 19:5*

Zacchaeus had three strikes against him—he had sold his allegiance to Rome and become a tax collector, he used his position to become very wealthy at other people's expense, and he was painfully aware that he was short.

And who did Jesus single out for a lunch appointment?

Great leaders are able to see beyond a person's past to their potential. They look for sparks of passion behind veils of misperception.

Perhaps Jesus saw a short, little man who had overcome tremendous odds. Maybe he sensed a heart longing to be generous beyond all expectation. Whatever it was, Jesus recruited Zacchaeus for his team.

How's your *special person* radar? Have you developed the ability to read between the lines of a person's résumé? Are you willing to risk hiring someone who breaks the mold?

❖ *Jesus hired Zacchaeus. Would you?*

Value Good Assistants

It is the bridegroom who marries the bride, and the best man is simply glad to stand with him and hear his vows. *JOHN 3:29*

It was the beginning of Jesus' ministry. Until now, John the Baptist had been the prevailing voice for change.

In the arena of public awareness, John the Baptist was at the top of his game. He was among the most famous people of his time, despite his odd diet and unusual fashion sense.

John also understood how to be a good Number Two.

John had a strong sense of his personal place in the scheme of things. He was aware of the important role he had been given and didn't try to elbow his way into an undeserved position.

Being a Number Two is not an easy role to fill. John wasn't an entry-level tagalong. He held his own in the spotlight, and when it came time to shine the light on someone greater, John was ready to remain active in the background.

❖ *Take a moment to think about your team. Do you have a good Number Two?*

Don't Look the Other Way

David and Abishai went right into Saul's camp and found him asleep, with his spear stuck in the ground beside his head. . . . "God has surely handed your enemy over to you this time!" Abishai whispered to David. "Let me pin him to the ground with one thrust of the spear." *1 SAMUEL 26:7-8*

A former CEO explained how he decided to make an investment that led to his company's demise.

> "The deal came out of nowhere, and we had to act quickly to take advantage of the opportunity before someone else did. I wish I hadn't looked the other way on a couple of points that didn't seem right."

There are certain boundaries you know you will never cross. For David, it was harming the man God had chosen to be king over Israel. Despite Saul's repeated attempts on David's life, David was not willing to negotiate this line in the sand.

❖ *Beware of opportunities that require you to look the other way—even if they appear to be tailor-made for your success.*

Allocate Resources Fairly

David said, "No, my brothers! Don't be selfish with what the LORD has given us. . . . We share and share alike—those who go to battle and those who guard the equipment." *1 SAMUEL 30:23-24*

Does your organization treat everyone fairly? Don't answer too quickly.

Does everyone receive a salary that is proportionate to the work they do? Are the staff restrooms just as nice as those in the executive wing? Do your top people get bonuses while their personnel are told there's no money for raises or additional help? What kind of car do you drive?

David's top soldiers had just wiped out the Amalekites, and God had allowed them to keep the treasure they had plundered. Some of the soldiers had stayed behind, and those who had gone into battle wanted to exclude them from sharing in the bounty.

David intervened and reminded his troops that the Lord had kept them safe.

❖ *If all provision comes from God, then we are merely God's agents. Are you handling God's finances in the way he would if he were sitting in your chair?*

Understand Cultural Diversity

Soon a Samaritan woman came to draw water, and Jesus said to her, "Please give me a drink."
JOHN 4:7

When advertisers first began to promote their products on Hispanic television stations, it was not uncommon to see an Anglo actor selling products with Spanish dubbed in over the original English. The graphics and music were directed at an Anglo audience, with the Spanish voice-over added afterward.

The ads spoke in Spanish, but they didn't address the cultural nuances of the audience they sought to attract. Most of them were ineffective.

Speaking the right language is the first step in communicating to a different audience. You need to understand the culture and the special sensitivities.

Jesus spoke to the woman in a language she understood, and she responded easily. He knew what was important to her, and she was comfortable with his approach.

How many diverse cultures do you work with? Age, language, geography, economics, education, religion, gender—each niche has a unique cultural language that will relate to your message in different ways.

❖ *Do you speak their language, or force them to understand yours?*

Do Your Personal Best

Pay careful attention to your own work, for then you will get the satisfaction of a job well done, and you won't need to compare yourself to anyone else. *GALATIANS 6:4*

I would rather be known for being *excellent* than for being the *best.*

Being the *best* is all about me. I am better than everyone else. I win and they lose.

Being *excellent* is about others. They benefit from my excellence. They win. It's not about me.

Which of these is closer to Paul's admonition?

+ We are going to sell more widgets than anyone else.
+ We are going to make the best widget on the market.

You needn't give up the first at the expense of the second, but giving up the second for the sake of the first is a sad case of misplaced priorities.

❖ *If you must compete, compete against yourself.*

Stop Telling Lies

Stop telling lies. . . . If you are a thief, quit
stealing. *EPHESIANS 4:25, 28*

Did Paul have twenty-first-century business practices
in mind when he wrote these words?

You are stealing if you

- let someone think you're giving them the best
    price when you know you would have gone
    lower, had they asked.
- use packaging that makes the product look bigger
    than it really is.
- buy one piece of software and use it on multiple
    computers.
- keep quiet upon realizing that a hotel or restau-
    rant has undercharged you for something.
- continuously put off that annoying salesperson,
    telling them you're still considering their offer,
    when you know for certain you're not going to
    buy anything.
- pay people less than they're worth because the job
    market is tight and they can't afford to leave.

❖ *If you are serious about honoring God in
your leadership, ask him to help you to "put
on your new nature, created to be like God"
(Ephesians 4:24).*

Play Your Own Game

I replied, "There is no truth in any part of your story.
You are making up the whole thing." They were just
trying to intimidate us, imagining that they could
discourage us and stop the work. So I continued
the work with even greater determination.
NEHEMIAH 6:8-9

The winning coach was interviewed after a game.

"Your guys were way behind at the half. What
did you say in the locker room that turned them
around?"

"I reminded them that we had a game plan and
that we should stop allowing the other guys to set
the pace. We came out and played our game, and we
won."

It is tempting to let the other team set your
agenda. Sometimes you unintentionally react to
something they're doing, take your eyes off the road,
and run into a ditch.

Nehemiah didn't blindly ignore the bad publicity his project was receiving, but neither did he let
it change his plans. He focused on getting the wall
built, and nothing got in his way.

❖ *The next time you're tempted to react, think
about Nehemiah and stay the course.*

Practice Proactive Transparency

What sorrow for those who say that evil is good
and good is evil, that dark is light and light is dark,
that bitter is sweet and sweet is bitter.   *ISAIAH 5:20*

My heart's desire as a kid was to save enough
money to send away for a pair of those X-ray glasses
advertised in the comic books. As I recall, none of
my friends ever got a pair. We were too skeptical or
too afraid that the glasses really would work and that
we would get into a world of trouble.

Here's a little secret: The people you're leading
don't need to order special glasses—they can see right
through you.

Learn to practice something I call proactive trans-
parency.
If you're sad, don't act happy.
If you're disappointed, say so.
When something tickles your funny bone, laugh
out loud.
If things aren't okay, don't say they are.

❖ *God laid out his case against Israel. High on
his list of offenses was their saying one thing
while meaning another. How do you score in
this area?*

Live Out Your Unique Purpose

Then Jesus explained: "My nourishment comes from doing the will of God, who sent me, and from finishing his work." *JOHN 4:34*

Allow me to paint a picture for you:

It's early morning in a home overlooking the Sea of Galilee. You can hear the sounds of the neighborhood as it begins to wake up. Jesus is sleeping on a mat in the corner. As a rooster crows and sunlight streams through a window in the east wall, he opens his eyes to meet the new day.

Is there any doubt in your mind that Jesus would have a smile on his face? Can you ever imagine Jesus moaning and pulling the covers over his eyes?

Jesus had an incredible lust for life.

The secret? He was doing exactly what God had placed him on earth to do. Jesus received so much strength from doing God's will that he referred to it as his nourishment.

The abundant life Jesus promises is possible when you understand and live out God's unique purpose for you.

❖ *Jesus woke with a smile on his face. Do you?*

Don't Play Favorites

Remember, you both have the same Master in heaven, and he has no favorites.   *EPHESIANS 6:9*

My computer's dictionary defines *double standard* as "a principle or expectation that is applied unfairly to different groups."

We seldom intend to play favorites. It just happens. For example,

> The policy manual prohibits staff from eating lunch at their desks, but busy executives do it when they have important calls that run through the lunch hour.
>
> Parents are encouraged to participate in their kids' school activities, but department heads are questioned if they leave early to catch a Little League game.
>
> Men with families are paid more than working moms, because a woman's wages are regarded as a family's second income.
>
> We talk about valuing our employees, but we fail to defend them when our best customer is a bully and treats them poorly.

❖ *It's all about mutual respect. God has no favorites and neither should you.*

Consider Everyone's Interests

Don't be selfish; don't try to impress others. Be humble, thinking of others as better than yourselves. Don't look out only for your own interests, but take an interest in others, too.   *PHILIPPIANS 2:3-4*

In baseball, one player may be asked to hit a sacrifice fly to advance another player into a scoring position. The batter hitting the sacrifice is *out* and doesn't have a chance to score a run, but he follows his manager's instructions for the good of the team.

I often suggest that my clients look for partnerships with other organizations to help them achieve their goals. In today's complex environment, it helps when multiple teams share resources to achieve common objectives.

As Paul tells us, we should work together with one mind and purpose.

Problems arise when one or more of the partners place their own goals ahead of the greater good. When that happens, I step in to remind everyone that insisting on their own interests will not get them as far as maintaining team spirit.

❖ *It's counterintuitive, but it works.*

Love Mercy, Truth, and Justice

God will establish one of David's descendants as king. He will rule with mercy and truth. He will always do what is just and be eager to do what is right.   *ISAIAH 16:5*

My clients will occasionally ask me to update their leaders on the state of employee satisfaction. It's an important exercise, and I applaud companies that don't take staff morale for granted.

More leaders should be proactive in this area. When a manager tells me that they're "doing okay in the HR department," I cringe, because quite often they're not.

When an employee survey turns up problem areas, a frequent response is to rationalize the issue. Changes are often granted reluctantly, and not before I hear how "some people need to realize they have it pretty good already."

Isaiah describes Jesus as a ruler who would be eager to do the right thing.

Think about your approach to employee satisfaction. On a sliding scale with *indifferent* at one end and *eager* at the other, where are you?

❖ *Are you anywhere close to where Jesus would be?*

Be a Party Animal

Go and celebrate with a feast of rich foods and sweet drinks, and share gifts of food with people who have nothing prepared.   *NEHEMIAH 8:10*

Contrary to conventional wisdom, Yahweh is quite a party animal.

All through the Old Testament, he encouraged the Israelites to celebrate, without being picky about the guest list. When the people had reason to be joyful, God wanted them to share with everyone—even those who came to the party unprepared.

When you have something to celebrate, bring as many people to the party as possible. Folks appreciate being part of a winning team.

Look for ways to thank each person who had a role in the project, even those who had nothing to do with the work, but will now enjoy the benefits.

Don't withhold your magnanimity. This isn't a time to boast or be self-important. It's a time to say, "We are excited, and we want to share our joy."

❖ *When there's good news to be celebrated, make your motto "The more the merrier."*

Look Beneath the Surface

Look beneath the surface so you can judge correctly.   *JOHN 7:24*

My friend Andy conducts a lot of business in Pacific Rim countries. One particular Chinese factory was causing him concern because he knew they were giving one of his competitors a much lower price on similar goods.

No matter what he tried, Andy's attempts to negotiate better terms met a closed door.

Then he learned this particular factory's boss was very traditional and refused to do business with anyone who did not come with a proper referral from a mutual friend. Once a formal introduction was arranged, the doors opened, and this factory is now one of Andy's top suppliers.

Jesus knew that a person's actions weren't always an accurate measure of their motives. If someone is doing something you don't understand or agree with, consider *why* they are acting as they are.

If you are facing a situation in which someone's actions seem uncooperative or hostile, explore the reasons for their behavior before writing them off.

❖ *Does your leadership tool kit include an ability to look beneath the surface?*

Invite Followers

Look! I stand at the door and knock. If you hear my voice and open the door, I will come in, and we will share a meal together as friends.   *REVELATION 3:20*

If anyone has a right to force his or her leadership ideas on others, it is Jesus.

I am struck by the patience he displays by simply standing at the door and knocking. He doesn't huff and puff and threaten to blow the house down.

He doesn't rattle the handle, shout, or demand to be let inside.

From the famous painting of *Christ at Heart's Door* by Warner Sallman, I get the sense that Jesus would prefer his host come to the door freely and without obligation.

You should lead in a similar manner. People who are coerced or otherwise obligated follow reluctantly and are more likely to abandon the cause if something else catches their fancy. If they stay, they do so halfheartedly, and you'll waste time keeping them motivated.

❖ *Do people follow you out of obligation or aspiration?*

Filter Your Reactions

These people scoff at things they do not understand. Like unthinking animals, they do whatever
their instincts tell them, and so they bring about
their own destruction. *JUDE 1:10*

I get a kick out of the patellar reflex.

When the hammer taps your kneecap, nerve
impulses race toward your brain, but they're short-
circuited at your spinal cord and rush back to make
your leg jump. The brain never gets a chance to
tell the leg not to make a fool of itself by jumping
uncontrollably.

Every organization has some people who behave in
a similar manner. They respond to ideas without first
filtering their reactions through their brains.

Knee-jerk critics are frustrating, but the good news
is that they are predictable.

Jude tells us these folks will "bring about their own
destruction." Perhaps he is referring to the disrespect
they bring on themselves as others grow weary of
their behavior.

❖ *The next time you float a new idea, stand
aside and let the automatic critics have their
moment. Then ask everyone else to engage
their brains and move forward.*

Fix Your Thoughts on God

You will keep in perfect peace all who trust in you, all whose thoughts are fixed on you! *ISAIAH 26:3*

It must have been when I was in elementary school. My dad was leading a Sunday night sing-along at the church, and he was teaching us a little chorus based on Isaiah 26:3.

Without warning, the whole building shuddered as something monstrous crashed through the front door. We rushed outside to find my dad's brand-new station wagon squeezed like an accordion between the building and the car that had slammed into—and totaled—it.

Dad gave the police the necessary information, but he couldn't wait to get back inside and finish the service. The car was demolished, and all he could think of was using the crash as an object lesson for the song he had been teaching.

❖ *This stuff isn't just theoretical; it really works. You will experience peace as a leader to the extent that you fix your thoughts on God.*

Take Roadblocks Seriously

"But I am the same donkey you have ridden all your life," the donkey answered. "Have I ever done anything like this before?" NUMBERS 22:30

Balaam had been riding his trustworthy donkey for many years, and he always got where he needed to go. Balaam trusted the donkey's abilities and judgment.

One day, the donkey was frightened by something and repeatedly shied away from the danger. Balaam became increasingly angry and jumped off the donkey's back to smack it on the nose.

It became a real-life *Mister Ed* episode when the donkey rebuked Balaam. He had seen an angel with a flaming sword blocking the road. When Balaam realized the donkey was trying to protect him, he begged forgiveness of the angel for going in the wrong direction.

You can expect some resistance to any new ideas, but pay attention in the rare instance when a trusted employee steers you clear of a chosen path. Ask him or her, "What do you see that I can't?"

❖ *Sometimes the stubborn one is the one who refuses to stop moving in the wrong direction.*

Do What Only You Can Do

Jesus knew that the Father had given him authority over everything and that he had come from God and would return to God. So he got up from the table, took off his robe . . . [and] he began to wash the disciples' feet.   *JOHN 13:3-5*

Take a pencil and circle the tiny word *so* in the middle of the passage.

In writing these daily devotions, God has given me fresh insight on some passages that I thought I knew fairly well. This is one of those instances.

Jesus was able to wash his followers' feet because he was secure in knowing that there were certain things only he could do. He told Peter, "Unless I wash you, you won't belong to me" (John 13:8).

We often get stuck on the foot washing and miss the deeper lesson, which is that there are some things that only a leader can do, such as setting vision, establishing standards, and praising a job well done.

As the leader, there are certain things only you are qualified to do.

❖ *Do you do them?*

Ignore People When Necessary

The Philistines became jealous of him. So the Philistines filled up all of Isaac's wells with dirt.
GENESIS 26:14-15

No matter how much you give back to the community, or how generous you are to your staff, or how hard you work to keep quality up and prices low, you are going to be criticized for your success.

The inevitability of jealous detractors doesn't excuse you from the need to be generous, but the reality of their perpetual existence should relieve you of the need to waste time trying to earn their approval.

It isn't about your success at all. It's about their lack of it.

Nothing you do to mitigate their jealousy will make a difference. If you try, you will be less successful because they will distract you from your mission—and they'll still be miserable.

Isaac was blessed with tremendous success. When Abimelech asked Isaac to leave, he didn't stay to argue his case. He just moved on.

❖ *Sometimes you need to ignore people. They will pose no real threat if you just leave them alone.*

Decide Whether to Fight or Switch

Abandoning that one, Isaac moved on and dug another well. This time there was no dispute over it. *GENESIS 26:22*

I don't know how wells were dug in those days, but I imagine it was a difficult task. Four times in a row, Isaac and his servants dug a well only to have it filled in or seized by local people.

It seems to me that Isaac would have been justified in resisting the appropriation of his hard work, but for some reason he decided each time to move on and dig another well.

As a leader, you need to know which battles to fight and which to ignore. Your decision will be influenced by your long-range plans. Your vision of the future will dictate whether you choose to fight or switch.

Isaac had set his sights on a place God had promised Abraham, and none of the abandoned wells were in this Promised Land. He was okay with giving them up and moving closer to his primary objective.

❖ *Knowing what you want tomorrow helps you decide what to do today.*

Hire a Good Publicist

If I were to testify on my own behalf, my testimony would not be valid. But someone else is also testifying about me, and I assure you that everything he says about me is true.   *JOHN 5:31-32*

Good PR firms and publicity agents are worth every dime you pay them.

PR people can say things about your organization that you would feel uncomfortable saying personally. When you say it, it sounds like hype. When the PR agent says it, it rings true.

News editors trust PR people who have proven their veracity. To modify the old E. F. Hutton slogan, when a good publicist talks, people listen.

Jesus knew the value of third-party endorsements. He knew that people would not be convinced by his word alone.

Perhaps you have considered engaging someone to manage your public image. Or maybe you're thinking of releasing your PR people to reduce expense. In either case, consider the leadership lesson Jesus provides in his description of John the Baptist's contribution to the mission.

❖ *Who tells your story?*

Control Your Attitude

Fix your thoughts on what is true, and honorable, and right, and pure, and lovely, and admirable. Think about things that are excellent and worthy of praise. *PHILIPPIANS 4:8*

Chuck Swindoll wrote a short, simple article titled "Attitude." It concludes with this phrase: "I am convinced that life is 10 percent what happens to me and 90 percent how I react to it."

There is so much that's beyond our control:
A supplier can suddenly raise prices or go out of business.
A valued employee can leave.
Government regulations can make your best product illegal.
Technology can make you obsolete.
Unforeseen circumstances can destroy everything you've worked for—leaving you with nothing except your attitude.

From the moment Jesus stopped Paul on the road to Damascus, Paul's life was out of his control. But he was in control of the one thing that mattered most—his thoughts.

❖ *The only thing that you can really control is your attitude.*

Take Your Time

You do such wonderful things! You planned
them long ago, and now you have accomplished
them.   *ISAIAH 25:1*

An entrepreneur is a person who wakes up with a
revolutionary idea and is disappointed when it hasn't
been implemented by lunchtime.

If that silly definition strikes close to home, you
aren't alone. Most of the visionary leaders I know
suffer the same frustration.

They have a vision, they take off with it, and the
rest of us scramble to catch up.

My friend Tim Blair calls it the rubber-band effect.
A rubber band is only useful when tension is applied
by stretching it. Tim says entrepreneurs are beneficial
because they stretch the rest of us.

If you're a real visionary, please don't stop. However, you may want to do yourself a favor by taking
a deep breath and considering that God, according
to Isaiah, takes great lengths of time to accomplish
things. He doesn't need the time, but *we* do.

❖ *The secret is not to stretch the rubber band
so far that it snaps.*

Don't Necessarily Finish Things

I replied, "But my work seems so useless! I have spent my strength for nothing and to no purpose. Yet I leave it all in the LORD's hand; I will trust God for my reward." *ISAIAH 49:4*

You are leading an organization, and your assignment is to keep your eyes on the horizon.

If you stop to finish something, you divert attention from the future and run the risk of missing an unexpected curve in the road.

Leaders lead. They don't necessarily finish things.

Isaiah was leading, but he couldn't see any results. His response was to trust God for his reward, and you should do that too.

On a practical level, you might do some tasks that you can finish, such as washing dishes or mowing the lawn. You might ask your team for regular updates and celebrate with them when they finish something. You could volunteer for something outside of work where you are not the leader.

❖ *God has given you a unique set of skills. Opening doors may be one; closing doors may not be.*

Try Out New Ideas

Please test us for ten days on a diet of vegetables and water.   *DANIEL 1:12*

People don't want to hear about change. They're afraid the new ideas will become permanent, even if they don't work.

If it ain't broke, don't fix it—and if it is broke, learn to live with it.

The man in charge of feeding Daniel and his friends a fat-rich diet was afraid the king would hear about their vegan regimen and have him beheaded. Daniel understood the concern and offered a solution—"We'll go back to the old menu if things don't work out."

If you are a change agent in your organization, most of the people you lead would rather leave things as they are. They don't look forward to getting up from their comfy chairs to try a new piece of furniture.

❖ *Ease them into a new idea by suggesting that they try it for a while. Make an honest evaluation at the end of the trial period and offer to go back if it doesn't work.*

Keep Your Eyes on the Lord

Don't let anyone think less of you because you are young. Be an example to all.   *1 TIMOTHY 4:12*

It's funny how perspectives change as we age.

When I was younger, I thought this verse meant that older people should give me a chance and shouldn't hold my youth against me.

Now that I'm sitting on the other side of the desk, I'm sure that Paul is telling younger members of the team to prove themselves by acting maturely.

I think both perspectives are correct.

Those of us with more experience should certainly not think less of our younger colleagues. They often supply fresh ideas and passion.

If you're just starting out, Paul encourages you to be an example for the rest of us. Don't expect us to hand over the keys without first showing us you can drive, but don't back off from sharing your excitement or bringing your stamina to the table.

❖ *We're never too young to lead and never too old to follow. Lead with your eyes on the Lord, regardless of your age.*

Earn People's Support

I am boldly asking a favor of you. I could demand it in the name of Christ because it is the right thing for you to do. But because of our love, I prefer simply to ask you. Consider this as a request from me. *PHILEMON 1:8-9*

Paul wanted Philemon to welcome home a man named Onesimus, who had been his slave but had run away. Onesimus was now a Christian, and he was returning to serve out his time. Paul wanted Philemon to receive his former slave as a brother, not as a servant.

Instead of pulling rank and demanding that Philemon follow his wishes, Paul appealed to his friend's sense of fairness and hoped that he would do what was right out of desire, not obligation.

You can demand that someone follow your lead or earn their support through mutual respect.

The first tactic produces a short-term victory.

The second lasts longer because it becomes their idea instead of yours.

❖ *Mercenaries make good soldiers, but lousy partners. Wouldn't you rather have followers who want to be there?*

Negotiate New Contracts

When God speaks of a "new" covenant, it means he has made the first one obsolete. It is now out of date and will soon disappear. *HEBREWS 8:13*

Contracts are a good idea. They spell out terms and expectations so there are no surprises. I sign contracts with all my clients, especially the ones I regard as good friends, because their friendship is valuable.

When writing a contract, I try to address everything that might occur during the assignment, but at times, changes are so substantial that it makes sense to rip up the old agreement and start from scratch.

New contracts shouldn't be entertained lightly. God's "new covenant" cost him dearly, but he knew it was the only way. His old agreement with the Israelites had been broken so many times that it was barely recognizable.

Although he could have stood his ground and demanded they honor their commitment, he knew the only way to save the project was to issue a new contract.

❖ *Going back to contract negotiation may cost you, but the result will be worth it.*

Slow Down before Deciding

Sarai said to Abram, "The LORD has prevented me from having children. Go and sleep with my servant. Perhaps I can have children through her." *GENESIS 16:2*

When my daughter and I watch *Wheel of Fortune,* we holler at the TV when a contestant blurts out a letter that has already been picked. I'm tempted to do the same with this story.

Abram, wait! Think about this. Yahweh himself has promised you a child through Sarai. Oh man, this is going to be trouble.

I have no empirical evidence for this, but I think the quality of a decision is directly related to the amount of long-range perspective you apply to the process.

Abram and Sarai were just looking at the immediate situation. They didn't understand that the effects of their choices that day would last for a long, long time.

Are you a problem solver? Are you always ready to jump in with a solution? The value of your contribution will be judged by the quality of the results, not the speed of your decision.

❖ *If you want to make better decisions, slow down.*

Make Things New

The faithful love of the LORD never ends! His mercies never cease. Great is his faithfulness; his mercies begin afresh each morning.

LAMENTATIONS 3:22-23

Human beings are extremely susceptible to what I call the Ho-Hum Factor.

We lose interest, become complacent, and often take important things for granted because they no longer sparkle with newness.

God understands this. He created us, and he knows us better than we know ourselves, so he renews his mercies every morning. His love for us never ceases, and he finds new ways to exhibit his care each day.

When was the last time you refreshed your messaging? Are you saying the same thing in the same way as you did a year ago? Have you updated your packaging or your logo?

If response to your last fund-raising appeal or sales flyer was disappointing, perhaps you need to find a new way to tell the story. People might be suffering from the Ho Hums.

❖ *God shakes the box every morning. How often should you do it?*

Lend a Helping Hand

Therefore, since we are surrounded by such a huge crowd of witnesses . . . .   *HEBREWS 12:1*

Derek Redmond was running the Olympic 400-meter race for Great Britain in the 1992 games.

As he rounded the final turn, the intense pain of a torn leg muscle brought him to the ground. With the crowd watching in disbelief, Redmond got up and started hopping on one foot toward the finish line.

That's when Jim Redmond, Derek's father, bolted out of the stands, pushed medics and security guards aside, and came to his son's assistance. Putting his arm around Derek's back, the elder Redmond walked with his son until he could cross the finish line.

The crowd went wild.

There are times when your role as a leader is to stand on the sidelines and cheer as your team accomplishes something. At other times, you'll be asked to leave your seat in the stands and help them finish the race.

❖ *Is there someone on your team who needs a helping hand?*

Be Slow to Speak

You must all be quick to listen, slow to speak, and slow to get angry. *JAMES 1:19*

There's a lot of *noise* these days.

It's not coming from those thumping boom boxes in the car next to you, or the guy yelling into his cell about his brother-in-law's psychiatric evaluation. It isn't your neighbor's lawn mower in the middle of your Sunday afternoon nap.

This noise results from a selfish desire to share our personal thoughts and opinions with the universe in a never-ending stream. We demand the first, last, and middle word in every conversation.

We are frequently angry, and we seldom wait for others to finish their sentences before spewing our responses at them. We are the antithesis of this scripture verse.

What if we led the way to a quieter world by

- keeping opinions to ourselves unless they actually add value to the dialogue?
- deciding never to have the first or last word in any dialogue?
- not contributing to the cacophony?

❖ *I imagine people would pay more attention when we did speak up.*

Know Where to Find the Answers

"It is beyond my power to do this," Joseph replied.
"But God can tell you what it means and set you at
ease." GENESIS 41:16

When I was a kid, everything I needed to know
could be found within the pages of the *Encyclopaedia
Britannica*. The world's collective knowledge was
there, and each year we received an update with new
knowledge.

Today, the world's knowledge base is expanding so
rapidly that it is impossible to keep up with everything in printed form. Before the ink dries on a page,
some of the information is out-of-date.

Since it is impossible to actually possess the latest
knowledge on a particular topic, it's no longer necessary to actually *know* anything. What is important is
knowing where to look for answers.

❖ *You need someone on your team who has an
insatiable thirst for knowledge and is constantly
looking for new sources of information. That
person should be able to say, "I don't know the
answer, but I know exactly where to go to find
out."*

Help People Glimpse the Future

Joseph's suggestions were well received by Pharaoh and his officials.   *GENESIS 41:37*

Joseph's story is a great example of the power we wield when we help people catch a glimpse of the future. To do that, we must share our dreams.

President Kennedy did it when he jump-started the space program. Dr. Martin Luther King Jr. did it at the Lincoln Memorial. Football coaches do it in pregame locker-room talks.

When you take people on a journey into the future, you give them hope as you lift their perspectives above the quiet desperation to which many are accustomed.

If you're a storyteller, practice and perfect your talent into a reliable strength. If you're not blessed with a visionary perspective, find someone who is and make him or her a member of your inner circle.

There is hope and fresh air in the future.

❖ *Help people see the future and they'll beg you to lead them toward it.*

Show Hospitality to Strangers

Don't forget to show hospitality to strangers.
HEBREWS 13:2

We all like to feel welcome.

One of the hotels I stay at has their computer system set up to recognize returning guests so the desk clerk can acknowledge them.

When my colleague and I arrived for an appointment at a large Southern California ad agency, our names were on a welcome screen in the lobby.

First-time visitors at our church receive a loaf of freshly baked bread when they stop at the information kiosk.

The early church was growing rapidly. You never knew who was or wasn't a believer, so the author of the book of Hebrews encouraged Christians to show hospitality to everyone.

How does your organization treat visitors and newcomers?

Do you have helpful signs so those unfamiliar with your facility can find their way around? Is your reception area inviting? Is your telephone answering system user friendly?

When Internet users visit your Web site, can they easily find what they're looking for, such as your phone number and mailing address?

❖ *How clean is your welcome mat?*

Make Some Phone Calls

I have much more to say to you, but I don't want
to do it with paper and ink. For I hope to visit you
soon and talk with you face to face.   *2 JOHN 1:12*

If you want to reduce the massive number of e-mails
you get, try responding to some of them with a
phone call rather than an e-mail.

E-mail is generally a good tool for communicating
with people who are not in the same room, but nothing beats the effectiveness of picking up the phone
and having a conversation in real time.

The apostles used letters and messengers to communicate, but they longed to hear the voices of their
friends and followers.

Try this experiment:

For the next seven days, respond to as many
e-mails as possible with a phone call.

Notice the reactions you get when people answer
the phone. My guess is that the majority of them will
be pleasantly surprised you took the time to dial their
number.

When it comes to effective communication, nothing beats the sound of a human voice.

❖ *Pick up the phone.*

Find a Spokesperson

Aaron will be your spokesman to the people. He will be your mouthpiece, and you will stand in the place of God for him, telling him what to say.
EXODUS 4:16

I've had the privilege of being an Aaron for a handful of great leaders who are better at making decisions and casting vision than they are at communicating.

In a few cases, I've been the public face of an organization. I have helped leaders write letters, press releases, and articles. It always begins with their asking, "Can you help me say what I mean to say?"

Spokespeople get a bad rap when they're used to protect public figures who are hiding from scrutiny, but when the motives are genuine, a well-trained mouthpiece can ensure the intended message is clearly stated.

Perhaps you're frustrated because the people you lead don't understand what you're saying.

❖ *A leader's responsibility is to lead. That's not easy to do if there's a breakdown in communication. Finding an Aaron might make all the difference in the world.*

Strengthen Your Weakest Link

So take a new grip with your tired hands and
strengthen your weak knees. Mark out a straight
path for your feet so that those who are weak and
lame will not fall but become strong.

HEBREWS 12:12-13

Leading people often requires you to stop talking
about the big picture while you guide your team
along the difficult paths that lie right at their feet.

Sometimes immediate issues are so overwhelming
that folks are discouraged by talk of *vision, future,*
and *long-range goals.* They don't know how to accomplish today's tasks, and thinking about tomorrow
makes them weary.

The Jewish Christians to whom the book of
Hebrews was written were hurting. They had been
struggling longer than any other group of believers,
and the light at the end of their tunnel wasn't shining
brightly. This passage urges their leaders to pay special attention to their weakest members.

Perhaps your team isn't making the kind of progress you'd like. Maybe they are falling behind. Your
best solution may be to put all the vision language
on hold and help them get past the obstacles in their
path.

❖ *Strengthen your weakest link.*

Don't Withhold Justice

In a lawsuit, you must not deny justice to the poor.   *EXODUS 23:6*

It makes for exciting TV drama, but the little guy seldom wins in court against a giant. We're drawn to such stories on TV, or in the movies, because we know they're a fantasy.

And the lesson extends beyond the courtroom.

As a leader, it is your responsibility to weigh every issue on its own merits, not on the strength of the presenter.

Senior staff members shouldn't be given preference over junior members of the team simply by virtue of having more tenure. Experience must have a voice, but experience is rooted in old ideas, and sometimes the best ideas come from people who are unaware of what was done before.

The Scriptures couldn't be more clear about this: Do what is fair, not what you can force on someone by virtue of your size, resources, experience, or your ability to hold your breath longer than anyone else.

❖ *Treat everyone fairly, regardless of their status or seniority.*

Do Something Different

Before the marriage took place, while she was still
a virgin, she became pregnant through the power
of the Holy Spirit.   *MATTHEW 1:18*

If your mission is to maintain the status quo, keep
doing exactly the same things in exactly the same
way.

But protecting the status quo is not what leadership is about. If the organization wants to stay where
it is, it doesn't need a leader. If you want to stay
where you are, you shouldn't be in leadership.

Leading involves taking people to places where
they haven't been before. To initiate change, you need
to *do things differently or do different things.*

God was about to initiate a dramatic change in his
relationship with mankind. He was on the verge of
smashing the status quo into a gazillion little pieces.

No virgin had *ever* conceived a child.

Have you been trying to build the future on
yesterday's ideas? Does your organization worship
the status quo?

❖ *Perhaps it's time to follow God's example
and try something new.*

Protect Your Reputation

Jesus sternly warned them, "Don't tell anyone about this." But instead, they went out and spread his fame all over the region.   *MATTHEW 9:30-31*

In the first-ever nationally televised presidential debate, Senator John Kennedy and Vice President Richard Nixon squared off in 1960.

The debate was carried on TV and radio. Those who watched TV generally thought Kennedy had won. Those who heard it on the radio gave the nod to Nixon.

Why?

Most analysts say that Nixon's not using makeup allowed viewers to see beads of perspiration on his upper lip, which gave him the image of insincerity. Kennedy won the image contest and ultimately the election.

Jesus knew that people would distort his message, so he sought to curtail the spread of his fame. He didn't hide the truth, but he understood the need to protect it from misinterpretation.

Your image is every bit as valuable as your real estate holdings, bank accounts, and inventory.

❖ *One of a leader's top priorities is the vigilant protection of their organization's reputation. How well are you doing?*

Don't Succumb to Grudge Holders

Ishmael's descendants . . . lived in open hostility
toward all their relatives.   *GENESIS 25:18*

In the mid-1990s, I managed a project that fell far
short of its projected results. None of the participants
lost money, but the benefits we promised never
materialized. It was a bust. I ran a full accounting
of the failure and reported everything to the
participants.

Most of them were disappointed, and some asked
tough questions. One man became unglued and
accused me of things that just weren't true. Nothing
I said calmed him down. Nothing my boss said eased
his tirade. Even his fellow participants tried to reason
with him, to no avail.

Like Ishmael, this individual continued to harbor
a grudge and refused to be involved in anything else
I was working on.

I gave up worrying about him a long time ago
because I realized that it wasn't a good use of the time
God has given me.

❖ *As a leader, you will encounter people who
hold grudges. Don't be drawn into their traps.*

Be Rich in Good Works

Tell [those who are rich] to use their money to do good. They should be rich in good works and generous to those in need, always being ready to share with others. *1 TIMOTHY 6:18*

A pastor friend of mine has a parishioner who is loaded.

Last week, this guy stopped by the church, handed one-hundred-dollar bills to everyone on the staff (it's a big church), and said, "You can do anything you want with this money, as long as it includes taking your spouse to a restaurant for a nice meal."

He doesn't stop with personal gifts. He has organized a group of wealthy friends who pool their resources to tackle bigger issues at the church.

You don't need to be wealthy to do good. Many people of lesser means make a difference with what they have, but Paul is speaking specifically to those who are financially successful.

Perhaps you have been blessed with more than you could possibly need. You are in a unique position to encourage others of similar circumstance to join you in good works.

❖ *Make the call.*

Finish Your Work

God, who began the good work within you, will
continue his work until it is finally finished.
PHILIPPIANS 1:6

The trouble with visionaries is that we see the ending
before we get there. We don't pay much attention
to details, so the last coat of paint doesn't always get
applied.

This lack of attention can be discouraging to the
folks who follow us. Their job is to get things done,
and when we don't show any interest in completing
the job, they wonder whether their work is appreciated or not.

Paul assured his readers that God can be relied
upon to finish what he starts. The lesson for leaders
is that we need to reassure people that we place a
high value on completed tasks.

If you have trouble crossing the finish line, find
someone you can rely on to bring the job home.
Celebrate enthusiastically when tasks are completed.

❖ *The only reason to begin a project is to enjoy
the benefit of having completed it.*

Change the Way You Think

Let God transform you into a new person by changing the way you think. ROMANS 12:2

At the end of Reggie McNeal's intense two-day seminar on the future of the church, my brain was tired. Reggie has more energy than a sack of wet cats, and listening to him talk about where God might be leading the church was physically and emotionally draining.

Rather abruptly, he slowed his pace, lowered his voice, and said he had one last question to ask. He warned us that the question would haunt us, then brought the slide up and just let it soak in:

"What has Jesus changed your mind about lately?"

My first reaction was, "Hey, that's easy. I'm an idea guy. I am always coming up with new ideas." But the more I pondered it, the more the question bugged me.

Paul isn't suggesting that I learn a new way to communicate with people. He isn't talking about the type of music I like or even the Bible translation I use.

❖ *Continued tomorrow . . .*

Let God Transform You

Let God transform you into a new person by
changing the way you think.   *ROMANS 12:2*

I change my mind about a lot of things. I have grown
accustomed to certain foods I once disliked. I have
altered my diet and exercise regimens. I now see
value in not wearing Hawaiian shirts to church every
week.

But Reggie McNeal's question—"What has Jesus
changed your mind about lately?"—ran deeper than
superficial personal preference or habit. He was urg-
ing a wholesale upheaval in my attitude regarding
things that really matter.

Letting Jesus change my mind was going to mean
a complete reversal in how I treated my employees,
set prices, and dealt with opportunity. Allowing Jesus
to change my mind would mean really loving people,
not just tolerating them.

Reggie was right. The Holy Spirit has been haunt-
ing me about this, and I'm still not sure I have an
answer. Perhaps the process is more important than
the destination.

❖ *As you make plans for next year, ask Jesus
what new ideas he has in mind for you.*

INDEX

FOCUS

FUTURE

HISTORY

INTEGRITY

WISDOM

About the Author

JIM SEYBERT has worked with leaders of small and large organizations, helping them think differently about what they do. His clients include entertainment and publishing giants, health-care providers, retailers, nonprofits, and real estate developers. In his free time, he likes to take deep breaths along the High Sierra trails of Yosemite National Park. For this book, Jim draws from years of experience as a corporate executive, small-business manager, and rank-and-file employee to provide insight into leadership principles.

To learn more about Jim Seybert, visit http://www.jimseybert.com

Do-able. <u>Daily.</u> Devotions.

START ANY DAY THE ONE YEAR WAY.

Do-able.
Every One Year book is designed for people who live busy, active lives. Just pick one up and start on today's date.

Daily.
Daily routine doesn't have to be drudgery. One Year devotionals help you form positive habits that connect you to what's most important.

Devotions.
Discover a natural rhythm for drawing near to God in an extremely personal way. One Year devotionals provide daily focus essential to your spiritual growth.

For Women

The One Year Devotions for Women on the Go

The One Year Devotions for Women

The One Year Devotions for Moms

The One Year Women of the Bible

The One Year Daily Grind

For Men

The One Year Devotions for Men on the Go

The One Year Devotions for Men

For Couples

The One Year Devotions for Couples

For Families

The One Year Family Devotions

For Teens

The One Year Devos for Teens

The One Year Devos for Sports Fans

For Bible Study

The One Year Life Lessons from the Bible

The One Year Praying through the Bible

The One Year through the Bible

For Personal Growth

The One Year Devotions for People of Purpose

The One Year Walk with God Devotional

The One Year at His Feet Devotional

The One Year Great Songs of Faith

The One Year on This Day

The One Year Life Verse Devotional

It's convenient and easy to grow with God the One Year way.

THE ONE YEAR WAY

Teach Truth.

MEET JESUS EVERY DAY THE ONE YEAR WAY.

For Kids

The One Year Devotions for Girls

The One Year Devotions for Boys

The One Year Devotions for Preschoolers

The One Year Devotions for Kids

The One Year Make-It-Stick Devotions

The One Year Bible for Kids: Challenge Edition

The One Year Children's Bible

The One Year Book of Josh McDowell's Youth Devotions